AMERICAN
IMMIGRATION

AMERICAN IMMIGRATION

Should the

Open Door

Be Closed?

BY GERALD LEINWAND

An Impact Book
FRANKLIN WATTS
New York ○ Chicago ○ London ○ Toronto ○ Sydney

Frontispiece: *A Lewis Hine photograph of an immigrant family on Ellis Island, 1905.*

Photographs copyright ©: New York Public Library, Picture Collection: pp. 8, 11, 27, 38, 41; Jacob A. Riis Collection, Museum of the City of New York: p. 43; The Ford Motor Company: p. 48; Chicago Historical Society: p. 51; National Archives, Public Health Services: p. 62; UPI/Bettmann: pp. 65, 78, 102, 105; The Bettmann Archive: p. 67; Reuters/Bettmann: pp. 83, 99; Archive Photos/Ron Sachs: p. 124.

Library of Congress Cataloging-in-Publication Data

Leinwand, Gerald.
American immigration : should the open door be closed? / Gerald Leinwand.
p.   cm.—(Impact book)
Includes bibliographical references and index.
Contents: A nation of immigrants, 1607–1820—Waves of immigration, 1820–1920—The closing door, 1920–1965—1965–1994, immigration resumes—Illegal immigrants and political refugees—Should the open door be closed?
ISBN 0-531-13038-X
1. United States—Emigration and immigration—Government policy.
2. Immigrants—Government policy—United States.   [1. United States—Emigration and immigration.]   I. Title.
JV6455.L524   1995
325.73'09—dc20   95-3303
                                                          CIP AC

CONTENTS

ONE OF MY SHARPEST MEMORIES ABOUT being a Cuban refugee was standing in line in downtown Miami's Freedom Tower with my family and hundreds of other newly arrived Cubans waiting to receive U.S. government-issued boxes of powdered milk, cheese and processed meat.

. . . Although I have come a long distance from that line . . . part of me is still there. The lines are now filled with Haitian and Nicaraguan faces, but on several occasions I would swear I've seen a little girl who looks just like me. May her thirty years in exile be as fulfilling as they have been for me.

—Ilena Ross-Lehtinen,
Florida Congresswoman
who became a U.S
citizen in 1972
Wall Street Journal,
July 3, 1990

PREFACE

WHY SHOULD I FEAR THE FIRES OF HELL?
I've been through Ellis Island.

Inscribed on the wall of Ellis Island[1]

Twenty-six million immigrants entered the United States between 1880 and 1924 when immigration was at its height and Ellis Island was the point of entry for nearly all of them. There were 2,500,000 Italians; 2,000,000 Austro-Hungarians; 1,800,000 Russians; 633,000 Germans; 551,000 English; and 348,000 Irish. They also came from Sweden (348,000), Greece (245,000), Norway (226,000), Turkey (212,000), and the West Indies (171,000). There were 2,500,000 Jews among them, making American Jewry the largest Jewish community in the world. Since 1820, some 57 million immigrants have come to America from over 155 countries. But these are mere numbers. The immigrants were men, women, and children, each with a story to tell. For all of them, coming to America was a defining moment in their lives. They came to a land that needed their labor and their skills but questioned their habits, life-styles, ways of worship, and foreign accents. Could such people ever really become American? Should America close its door? These questions were asked and asked again in each generation.

In 1924 American immigration laws reduced to a trickle the flow of newcomers. By 1954 Ellis Island had been shut altogether, and in 1965 it became part of the National Park Service. In 1982 private funds were solicited to turn it into a museum as a tribute to those immigrants who, undaunted by the obstacles they faced, made a life for themselves in America even as they helped to make America. Today Americans in search of their roots come to Ellis Island.

A ferry takes the tourist to surroundings that offer a taste of what it was like to be herded, labeled, tagged, interrogated, and to be physically examined for signs of deformity, tuberculosis, and other contagious diseases. Sometimes the immigrants were verbally assaulted by overworked immigration officers who were frustrated by the language barriers that made communication difficult despite the availability of interpreters. At other times the new arrivals were prodded and poked by doctors and nurses who had little regard for their modesty or privacy. A chalk mark on a person's jacket, or a tag—*B* for a back ailment; *L* for lameness; *C* for conjunctivitis and *Ct* for trachoma, two contagious eye diseases; or *Pg* for pregnancy—could mean that an immigrant would be returned to the land where the journey had begun. About 2 percent of the newcomers were sent home, and one in five was held in detention until the officials were satisfied that he or she could be legally admitted.

First- and second-class passengers could bypass the Ellis Island experience. These privileged groups could go through the immigration process aboard ship, leave as soon as formalities had been completed, and be on their way to begin their lives in America. Those who came third class, in steerage—so called because the cramped and often unsanitary accommodations were located near the steering mechanism—however, were forced to wait until tenders would ferry them from the ocean liner to Ellis Island.

Too frequently the immigrants' few possessions and limited cash were stolen. Predators took advantage of the immigrants' lack of English and promised, for a fee, to find them housing, jobs, or relatives, promises they had no intention of keeping. Of her experiences on Ellis Island, where she arrived in 1927, Immaculata Cuomo, mother of

Immigrants on Ellis Island, circa 1905.
In the years from 1892 to 1924, more than
12 million people came through Ellis Island.

former New York governor Mario Cuomo, said: "It wasn't always a happy memory."[2] Her words reflect the experiences of many who passed through Ellis Island.

Since 1965 immigration to America has resumed, but the majority of immigrants arrive neither by ship nor from Europe, and Ellis Island is no longer the processing point for immigrants. Instead, today's immigrants travel in giant 747 airplanes to New York, Chicago, San Francisco, Miami, Houston, and other cities. The new immigrants come from Asia, Africa, and Latin America. But today, as then, some Americans are concerned about the nation's ability to absorb the newcomers.

AMERICA REMAINS A LAND
OF IMMIGRANTS

Today only 6.2 percent of the American population is foreign born. This is about half the figure for 1930, but far higher than it had been for the previous thirty years.[3] While America is the most popular destination for immigrants, other countries have a much larger percentage of people who have been born in another country. For example, 20.9 percent of those living in Australia were born abroad, as were 8.2 percent of those living in Canada, and 7.6 percent in Germany. But in terms of numbers, rather than in terms of percent, the United States has the largest immigrant population in the world.[4]

And yet many Americans rarely see an immigrant. While we speak of the United States as a "nation of immigrants," the fact is that immigrants are concentrated in a few areas of the country. Nearly 82 percent of the immigrants in this country live in the large cities of California, New York, Texas, Illinois, and Florida. This concentration of immigrants helps to explain why some Americans feel that they're surrounded by strangers, fear that immigrants are taking jobs from them, worry about high crime rates, feel concerned about alleged deterioration of the schools their children attend, or doubt that the immigrants can ever be assimilated into the mainstream of the population. There is often concern in these high-concentration areas that immigrants use a disproportionate share of welfare and food stamps, or that they swamp the emergency rooms of hospitals. Even though immigrants are concentrated in some urban areas, immigration affects the nation as a whole. In the last decade of the twentieth century, Americans appear to have a renewed interest in closing the door to further immigration and in turning their backs on a long tradition. According to a 1992 Gallup poll, 69 percent of Americans interviewed felt that too many immigrants were coming from Latin America. Six in ten Americans (58 percent) felt that too many were coming from Asia, while 47 percent felt that too many were coming from Africa. Only 36 percent believed that too many European immigrants were coming. A Gallup poll taken ten years earlier indicated substantially less concern about the number of new arrivals.[5]

A New York Times-CBS poll in 1993 revealed that 61 percent favored a decrease in the number of immigrants entering the country. This contrasts with the results of a poll taken in 1986, in which only 49 percent favored a decrease. In 1977 only 42 percent favored reducing immigration, and in 1965 only 33 percent called for a decrease.[6]

In New York City, where 2.1 million, or 28 percent of the city's population, is foreign born, 63 percent of those surveyed by telephone believed that the number of recent immigrants to the city was too high. About 60 percent of those queried believed that immigrants were having a negative effect on the city. Even some immigrants themselves held such views. Large percentages of American-born and foreign-born residents believe that the bombing of the World Trade Center in New York would not have taken place if there had been tighter controls on immigration.[7]

Once again the people of America are debating whether or not to close the open door.

NATION OF IMMIGRANTS
1607–1820

ON JUNE 10, 1940, WHEN WE STEPPED OFF
the SS *Manhattan* in New York we were greeted
by our cousins. . . . Irene took one look at my
straight hair and bangs, and declared in her
heavily accented Bronx English, "Mudlin, this is
America. You gotta have coils. In America, all
the goils have coils. . . ." My mother, who
brought her two children to America alone . . .
gave us the vision of the American dream. Quite
simply she believed it. Anything was possible
in America.

> —Madeleine Kunin, former governor of Vermont
> and currently deputy secretary of education
> in the Clinton Cabinet, born in Zurich
> and became a U.S. citizen in 1947[1]

President Franklin D. Roosevelt, speaking before the
Daughters of the American Revolution, a conservative
group of women who trace their ancestry to the American
Revolution, addressed them as "fellow immigrants." His
audience was not amused. Yet FDR was right. Americans
are almost all immigrants or descendants of immigrants.
Many American families have stories to tell of how they
got to the United States. Immigration is the collective story

of how Americans arrived, how they fared, and how they changed America and were changed by their adopted land.

Not all immigration was voluntary. African-Americans were enslaved and forced to come to the New World. Other immigrants were driven by economic hardship, religious or political persecution, or war to leave their homelands.

In the United States, the Inuit and the American Indian are the only clearly native Americans. Yet, in the opinion of some anthropologists, even the Indians of continental United States are immigrants.

THE AMERICAN INDIAN AS IMMIGRANT

In their pursuit of animals for food and furs, the Mongolian aboriginal ancestors of the American Indians crossed the Bering Strait, which was then a land bridge between Asia and America, sometime between 30,000 B.C. and 12,000 B.C. When Columbus made his first journey to the New World in 1492, there were about 20 million human beings living between the Aleutian archipelago of Alaska, the Atlantic coast, and the southern tip of South America. These peoples had developed their own religious practices, diverse cultures, and about nine hundred different languages. When the first Europeans reached the New World there were almost 900,000 Indians, organized into 2,000 tribes, in the area that was to become the United States.

It became the policy of the new United States after 1830 to drive the Indians from their own lands because the European immigrants sought to settle and cultivate them. Treaties with the Indians were made and broken as were the many promises to recognize their claim to the lands they occupied. In two hundred costly wars ruthlessly conducted by a government that cared little about the original inhabitants, the Indians were forced to give up their lands and go to live on government controlled reservations. Those

Indians who were not assimilated suffer to this day as a result of this ill-conceived policy.

THE HISPANIC
AS IMMIGRANT

Although the traditions and institutions of the United States were shaped by the English conquest and settlement of the coast of the North American continent, it is important to remember that in 1513—nearly a century before the first English settlement was founded at Jamestown, Virginia, in 1607—the Spanish had established a colony in Saint Augustine, Florida. By 1574 there were two hundred Spanish cities and towns in North and South America. The cities in the American Southwest that were established by Spanish settlers include San Diego (1542), Santa Fe (1605), San Francisco (1776), and Los Angeles (1781). The American Southwest received much of its character from the Spanish and Mexican traditions.

THE AFRICAN
AS IMMIGRANT

The first black to come to America arrived with Columbus. Thirty blacks marched with Balboa when he crossed the isthmus of Panama in 1513. Three hundred blacks were in the service of Cortez when he conquered Mexico in 1519. Blacks served with Pizarro when he conquered Peru in 1531, and blacks helped build Saint Augustine, Florida, the oldest city in the United States. Some blacks, like Stephan "Estevanico" Dorantz, became important explorers in their own right. Estevanico, which means "Little Stephan," is credited with being the first to explore Arizona and New Mexico. But ten years after Columbus discovered America, King Charles V of Spain recognized African blacks as legitimate items of trade and gave favored courtiers the right to trade in slaves with the West Indies and later with North and South America.

In 1619, before the *Mayflower* landed in Plymouth, the first blacks arrived in Jamestown, Virginia, and were sold to planters as indentured servants. Indentured servants agreed to work without pay for a number of years in exchange for relief from their indebtedness or for their transportation to the New World. Many whites as well as blacks initially came to America in this way. However, as labor shortages developed in the colonies, enslavement of blacks became the rule and slavery became one of the earliest institutions developed in the American colonies. It was not long before traffic in slaves became an important part of the colonial economy.

The horrors of the middle passage—the sea route taken by slave ships—are almost impossible to describe and almost beyond imagining. Slaves were chained below deck, and forced to lie spoon fashion in close proximity to one another. With but eighteen inches above their heads they could neither sit nor stand unless they were taken above deck for air and exercise. If the vessel hit a storm or was becalmed along the way, conditions became more intolerable still. Tropical heat, seasickness, scurvy, and smallpox killed many. So foul were the slave ships that they could sometimes be smelled before they were seen. Many slaves died en route and others were too sick upon arrival to be sold. Yet, with profits of sometimes over 500 percent, the slave trade was enormously profitable for traders and all the intermediaries who participated in the traffic of human chattels.

By 1776 there were over 500,000 slaves in the American colonies, which then had a population of 2,500,000. While slaves could be found in all the colonies, it was in the southern colonies that slavery became a fundamental institution that would have grave consequences for the emerging nation. By the last quarter of the eighteenth century slaves formed two-fifths of the population of

Virginia, about two-thirds that of South Carolina, and more than one-third that of Georgia.

In the American colonies whites who came as indentured servants eventually earned their freedom. Harsh though their servitude may have been, as whites they retained all political and legal rights of the colony and, later on, of the new nation. When their period of indenture was over, they became citizens in every sense of the word. They could travel where they wished and accept such employment as they preferred.

The slaves, however, were bound for life, as were their children. While slavery in the middle and northern colonies eventually died out, slavery in the southern colonies became entrenched by law, tradition, custom, and racial prejudice. It seemed to be an easy and cheap solution to the chronic shortage of labor in the American colonies. Easily identified by the color of their skin, they could not readily escape. The courts of law, the privileges of citizenship, the right to own property, to become literate, to have marriages legally recognized were all denied them. No slave could leave a plantation without written permission of the owner. Slaves wandering around without such permission could be captured and returned. Slaves thought guilty of murder or rape were hanged. For minor offenses slaves were whipped, maimed, or branded. For theft, slaves were given sixty lashes by the sheriff and bound in a pillory with their ears nailed to the posts for half an hour; then their ears were cut off.

Those slaves who worked as field hands, house servants, skilled carpenters, bricklayers, or unskilled workers often rebelled against their masters. While they knew they could not prevail, they did succeed in heightening the tension so that no master could feel completely secure. "Before the end of the colonial period Virginia, like her neighbors, had become an armed camp in which masters figuratively kept their guns cocked and trained on the slaves in order to keep them docile and tractable."[2] Thus slavery held both blacks and whites in bondage.

According to the Constitution of the United States, the slave trade—but not slavery itself—was to end in 1808, and in that year the legal traffic in slaves was terminated. Until the outbreak of the Civil War in 1861, however, slaves were regularly smuggled into the United States. Also, while slaves could no longer be legally imported from Africa, a brisk domestic trade in slaves continued among the states. Slave families were not recognized under law, and so children could be readily separated from their parents, and wives from husbands, when their owners sold them.

Because slaves could no longer be legally imported, the cost of those that were smuggled into the country rose sharply, with the result that agitation mounted for the legal reopening of the slave trade. Said one southern senator in arguing for the reopening of the slave trade, "If it is right to buy slaves in Virginia and carry them to New Orleans, why is it not right to buy them in Cuba, Brazil, or Africa?" In his view, it was unfair for the South to be denied access to the enormous pool of slave labor available in Africa while the North had access to European labor through unrestricted immigration.

The enslavement of blacks is the fault line in American history. Though the injustice of slavery was recognized by many in the North as well as the South, race prejudice was such that few felt that blacks and whites could ever successfully live together as equals. Thomas Jefferson, the framer of the Declaration of Independence and third president of the United States, recognized that slavery was basically evil and that it would threaten the nation he had so large a role in founding. Although he was a slave owner who shared the racist prejudices of his day, he wrote, referring to slavery, "I tremble for my country when I reflect that God is just; and that his justice cannot sleep forever."

IMMIGRATION TO COLONIAL AMERICA
1607–1776

In his *Letters from an American Farmer*, Michel Guillaume Jean de Crèvecoeur (1735–1813) wrote: "What then is the American, this new Man . . . ? He is an American, who leaving behind all his ancient prejudices and manners receives new ones from the new mode of life he has embraced, the new government he obeys, and the new rank he holds." But a distinctive American was slow in emerging. Originally, all colonists who came from England viewed themselves simply as English people who lived in America. But as early as 1691, the Reverend Cotton Mather used the term "American" to designate the special kind of people who lived in the New World. In the early eighteenth century, the term "American" was used with derision by the sophisticates of England and the Continent. Those who lived in the British colonies were mockingly called Americans in much the same way as urban people today sometimes refer to those living in the country as yokels. Benjamin Franklin reported that to Europeans, the American was still understood "to be a kind of 'yahoo.'"

In 1776, Patrick Henry (1736–1799) declared to the Continental Congress, "I am not a Virginian but an American!" By 1787, when the Founding Fathers gathered at Philadelphia to write a constitution for the nation, Charles C. Pinckney of South Carolina advised those assembled that Americans were neither English nor European but a distinctive people.

The distinctive characteristic of colonial Americans was diversity. Although the dominant stream remained English, the colonists came from many countries, practiced a variety of religions, and spoke different languages. Many spoke English only with great difficulty. For example, for fifty years the Dutch colony of New Netherlands—later New York—divided the colonies along the colonial seaboard. There were large settlements of Scotch-Irish, Germans, Huguenots (French Protestants). Small groups of Jews, mainly from Spain and Portugal, lived in Rhode Island and in New York, with a scattering in other places.

Most of the relatively few Catholics were clustered in Baltimore, Maryland. Swedes were in present-day Delaware. Large numbers of Germans lived in Pennsylvania together with Finns and Danes. Numerically, the Scotch-Irish and Germans were the largest groups, and many early settlers were already voicing their fear that the character of America would be undermined if unrestricted numbers of German immigrants were allowed entry. When to this ethnic mixture one added Native Americans and African-Americans, one can understand why colonial America is sometimes described as a mosaic of people.

While those who came to America were not the most prosperous people of Europe, they were nevertheless able at least to scrape together some meager resources to pay their passage and to sustain themselves until they could buy land, go into business, or get a job. Large numbers came as indentured servants who worked off their debts and passage by working as farm laborers, craftsmen, domestic servants, or teachers. While they brought limited wealth, they were not the dregs of European society. Most of them could read and write, and they were skilled enough to contribute to the development of the emerging nation while earning a decent living.

The Middle Atlantic colonies had the most diverse population. The New England colonies were seemingly the most homogeneous, with white Anglo-Saxon Protestants (Congregationalists, Methodists, Presbyterians) predominating. In the southern colonies Anglicanism was practiced by the whites.

Despite these differences, there were important commonalities among the colonists. Although there were many sects, Protestantism was the dominant religion. The existence of numerous religious groups encouraged religious toleration although there were some exceptions. While forms of colonial government varied and suffrage (voting rights) was limited, all had representative legislatures whose members were relatively freely chosen by the voters.

WHY THEY CAME

Early immigrants were both pushed and pulled to the New World. The push came from conditions in Europe that some immigrants found intolerable. In Europe, all people lived under the rule of all-powerful monarchs and a landed nobility. Most people lived and died in the same economic class in which they were born. They could not acquire land because all was the property of the local lord. They were subject to an unfair system of taxation that imposed heavier burdens on the poor and powerless than on the rich and powerful. Some immigrants sought to escape such difficult conditions.

Under the rule of primogeniture in England, only the oldest son could inherit the estate of a parent. Many younger sons of the nobility perceived that the New World offered greater opportunity for them to make their fortune.

Religious intolerance also pushed the oppressed to pull up stakes; forsake family, friends, and community; risk a sea voyage of many weeks; and plant new roots in America. They wanted to leave a country that inhibited the expression of their religious beliefs or explicitly persecuted them. In all countries of Europe either Catholicism or Protestantism was the religion of the state, and those who did not conform to the religion of the monarch were often harshly treated. In the New World, while there were flare-ups of religious fanaticism and prejudice against Quakers, Jews, and Catholics, there was also substantial religious freedom and toleration. Eventually freedom of religion was written into the Bill of Rights.

Some early European immigrants were forced to emigrate. England, during the eighteenth century, sent some 30,000 convicts to the New World. In order to meet the demand for cheap labor, children of the poor were sometimes kidnapped and forcibly taken to the New World by unscrupulous shipowners who sought to recoup the cost of the journey from employers who needed laborers.

The pull came from real or imagined opportunities for religious liberty as well as for economic opportunity. For many, it was not so much that conditions in Europe were so bad for them, as that they were drawn to America because of its freshness and novelty. The spirit of adventure, the lure of freedom, vaguely defined, the search for tranquility, the release from boredom, the yearning for liberty, were all among the factors encouraging early migration to colonial America. Some were drawn to America because they thought that they could make a fresh start and make money. In 1680 fewer than 200,000 people were living in colonial America. Because there was an enormous need for labor, many colonies offered substantial inducements to Europeans to come and settle, particularly to those who professed the Protestant faith. One important inducement was the so-called headright system in which land was granted to wealthy patrons when they sponsored settlers by paying their fare to America. In some colonies immigrants were exempted from taxation for a period of years. Other colonies helped immigrants pay the cost of their transportation, or helped new arrivals get settled with a grant of free tools, provisions, and even land.

Sometimes immigrants were especially well rewarded for settling in hazardous locations on the frontiers where they could protect the colonies from French and Indian attacks. The southern colonies had to offer particularly generous inducements to white settlers. These colonies were sparsely settled, the climate was considered unfavorable, and many Europeans were reluctant to begin a new life as slaveholders or to live in a colony with large numbers of enslaved people.

Wide-ranging publicity in London painted a bright picture of life in colonial America. Free or cheap land, religious toleration and relatively low taxes were all advertised in newspapers and pamphlets and even from the pulpits. Letters from emigrants to those back home were an important incentive that gradually increased the flow of immigrants to the New World.

EARLY RESTRICTIONS ON IMMIGRATION

Even in the colonial period there was friction between earlier immigrants and those who came later. Roman Catholics were discouraged from settling in some colonies, although they were not actually prohibited from doing so. Those who seemed unable to support themselves were also often unwelcome.

Emigration policies played a role in the conflict between England and the colonies. Parliament failed to understand, among other things, the desire of the colonies to have England encourage a more open policy of emigration. Emigrants to America from non-English-speaking nations were not eligible for naturalization as British citizens. As a result, those who came to colonial America but were not British subjects had no assurance that their rights would be protected. Essentially they were people without a country. Some colonies did pass laws making non-British settlers citizens, but these laws were not recognized by the Crown.

In 1740, however, Parliament did pass a law making naturalization possible for those who had previously been ineligible for citizenship. Those seeking British citizenship were required to show that they had been living in the colonies for seven years and that they were loyal to the monarch. They also had to give evidence of their Protestant Christian faith (except those who were Quakers or Jews). Catholics could not become citizens under these provisions. The legislation of 1740 was little used because the residency period was fairly long. Moreover, because Parliament in 1760 and again in 1773 had made naturalization of aliens even more difficult, the framers of the Declaration of Independence included the following complaint among their grievances against the king: "He has endeavored to prevent the population of these states; for that purpose obstructing the Laws for Naturalization of foreigners, refusing to pass others to encourage their migration hither, and raising the conditions of new Appropriations of Lands."

When the United States Constitution was being drafted there was considerable debate about whether there should be an open or restricted immigration policy. Alexander Hamilton (1757–1804) of New York, a West Indian by birth, and George Mason (1725–1792) of Virginia, favored the open policy while Gouverneur Morris (1752–1816) of Pennsylvania favored the restricted policy. Article I, Section 8, of the Constitution authorizes Congress "to establish a uniform rule of naturalization." And James Madison, in *The Federalist* papers, cited this provision as an important reason to adopt the new Constitution.[3]

The Constitutional Convention agreed that only the presidency would be limited to the native born. Senators would have to have been citizens for nine years and representatives for seven. Both James Madison and Alexander Hamilton believed that religious liberty would be the single most important attraction of the new nation to the foreign born. Clearly the framers of the Constitution expected immigrants to make a major contribution to the new United States.

IMMIGRATION AND THE NEW NATION

What to do about immigrants may be thought of as the longest debate in the nation's history. From the earliest days, the new nation was confronted with the question of how best to deal with immigrants from abroad. It was not that the United States was the only nation to be peopled by immigrants, but it was a country which served as a magnet to attract immigrants from many lands. Of the millions of people who have migrated from Europe to other countries, about two-thirds went to America. Four-fifths of the immigration to Australia came from Britain. Italy and Spain furnished three-quarters of the immigrants to Argentina, while nearly all immigrants of the Union of South Africa came from Britain or Holland. "The massive transfer to the Western Hemisphere," wrote Bernard Bailyn, the distinguished historian of American social history, "from Africa, from the European mainland, and above all from the Anglo-Celtic offshore islands of Europe culminating in what Bismarck called 'the decisive fact of the modern world,' is the peopling of the North American continent."[4]

Because labor was so desperately needed, the recently established Congress passed legislation to encourage emigration from Europe. The legislators required only that free white aliens who sought citizenship in the new nation renounce any other allegiance and live in America for two years. However, emigration to America was slow, as the nations of Europe sought to discourage the widespread exodus of their people. The hazards of continuing warfare between France and England and their allies made travel by land and sea even more treacherous than it ordinarily was. Between 1783 and 1815 only 250,000 immigrants came to the new nation. During some years as many as 10,000 new immigrants reached America, but the number was sometimes as low as 3,000. During the War of 1812

Many immigrants in the colonial period were craftsmen, such as these New England shipbuilders.

between the United States and England, the flow of immigration nearly ceased.

If, during the early years, the quantity of immigrants was small, the quality was unusually high. Among them was John Jacob Astor (1763–1848), who built his fortune by developing the fur trade. Phyllis Wheatley (1753–1784) came as a slave from Africa and became the best-known female poet in America. Albert Gallatin (1761–1849) came from Switzerland and eventually became a distinguished secretary of the treasury. Éleuthère Irénée Du Pont (1771–1834), seeking to escape the French Revolution's Reign of Terror, came to America and became a leading industrialist. Although England refused to share its technical developments with the new nation, the Englishman Samuel Slater (1768–1835) in 1789 came to Pawtucket, Rhode Island, where, from memory, he set up the first cotton factory in America.

The American government wanted the new settlers to carve farms out of the wilderness, but the majority preferred to seek their fortune in the the growing cities of New York, Baltimore, Boston, and Philadelphia. In these urban centers the new immigrants learned English and were gradually assimilated into the mainstream of the population.

It was not long before considerable concern arose among the people that refugees from the French Revolution, from the Napoleonic Wars (1789–1815), and from rebellion in Ireland were bringing political zealots to the New World. Fear that these newcomers would would fan the flames of discontent, conspire to draw America into war with one or more European nations, or serve as spies for America's potential enemies led to an intense but short-lived effort to protect the nation from dangerous aliens.

In 1795 the residency waiting period for white aliens was extended from two years to five years. In 1798, the Naturalization Act extended the required period of residence prior to becoming eligible for citizenship from five to fourteen years. The Alien and Sedition Acts gave the president the authority to expel by executive decree any foreigners who were suspected of being a danger to the nation. While President John Adams (1797–1801) made very limited use of these powers, expelling only two Irish journalists, the legislation showed that foreigners could not be assured of remaining in the United States.

American immigration policy was, from the outset, erratic. The nation welcomed and needed the labor and the skills of newcomers, yet bigotry, prejudice, and fear made many Americans nervous about their foreign accents, strange clothing, ethnic foods, and religious practices.

Despite these reservations, with the election of Thomas Jefferson as third president of the United States (1800–1808) the Alien and Sedition laws expired, and the Naturalization Act was modified so that an immigrant had to wait only five years, rather than fourteen, to apply for citizenship. Thus the stage was set for one of the great periods of American immigration.

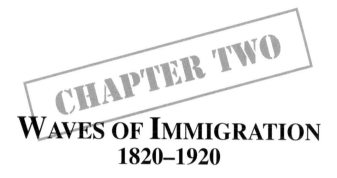

WAVES OF IMMIGRATION
1820–1920

IT'S BEEN MORE DIFFICULT THAN I THOUGHT.
[But] There are more opportunities here; there,
people look out for you. After a while I'll feel
better. Especially after I learn English. After I
begin school. I like to study and that's the best
way to progress.

—Asenhat Gomez,
an eighteen-year-old
from the Dominican
Republic who arrived
in the United States
in May 1992[1]

In describing the immigration to America between
1820 and 1920, the metaphor of the wave is often used.
Immigration is compared to the waves of the sea that crash
upon one another as they reach the shore. In speaking of
an Irish or a German wave of immigration, reference is to
the dominant group that came at that particular time. It is
the dominant group that gave each wave of immigration
its special character and elicited a unique response from
those Americans already arrived.

The German poet Johann Wolfgang von Goethe
(1749–1832) wrote: "America you have it better than our
continent, the old one." And, since the founding of the
American republic, many from the "old" continents of
Europe, Africa, and Asia have agreed with him. Between

1815 and 1860 some 5 million European immigrants, mainly from Great Britain, Ireland, and Germany, came to America, a number greater than the entire population of the United States in 1790, when the first census was taken. In the single decade between 1845 and 1854, approximately 3 million immigrants arrived, representing about 15 percent of the total American population of about 20 million. "According to the census of 1905, in a total white population of 135,000,000, the foreign-born and persons of foreign or of mixed parentage amounted to 33,750,653, or exactly 25 percent of the total."[2] America, during those years, provided a haven for the largest proportion of immigrants the nation has ever witnessed. Emigrants looked toward the New World as a land of opportunity. In the mid-nineteenth century this was particularly true for the Irish and the Germans. Whole communities uprooted themselves in what became known as the "American fever" and sought their Garden of Eden in America.

Those in the first wave of mass migration came mainly from northern and western Europe, and historians have described these men, women, and children as the old immigrants. Those who came from southern and eastern Europe historians have described as the new immigrants.

THE OLD IMMIGRANTS
1820–1890

Irish Immigrants Kate Kennedy of County Meath emigrated from Ireland with her brother and sister during the potato famine of 1848. To make a living in the United States they embroidered cloaks and vests, and with money saved from their wages they brought over their mother and four other sisters. At the same time Kate went to school. By 1857, less than ten years after coming to America, the family had been reunited. They resettled in San Francisco, where Kate taught school and became a principal. All of

Kate's sisters also became teachers, and Kate Kennedy went on to become a trade union advocate demanding equal pay for equal work and an end to salary discrimination against women.[3]

While not all immigrants met with success, a common thread running through the history of immigration is the achievement of improved living standards at least by the second and third generations. Although Kate Kennedy was more fortunate than most, a study of Irish immigrants reveals why and how successive waves of immigrants sought refuge in America.

In 1801, according to the terms of the Act of Union, the Irish Parliament was dissolved and Ireland was ruled entirely by the British Parliament. Although Ireland sent representatives to Parliament they were ineffective in getting Parliament to resolve Irish grievances. By 1829, however, when the Catholic Emancipation Act was adopted and Catholics could represent Ireland in Parliament, a group of Irish Protestants and Catholics kept up pressure on Parliament to ease the harsh rents exacted by absentee English landowners on Irish tenant farmers, to remove the tax imposed on Catholic Ireland to pay for the Protestant Anglican church, and to give the Irish a greater voice in their own government. But England was slow in responding to Irish needs.

Ireland was the most densely populated country in Europe and the natural resources of the country could not sustain an Irish population of about 8 million. Between 1820 and 1850 conditions in Ireland were especially difficult. Most Irish were small farmers who did not own their own land. Instead, they paid exorbitant rents to absentee English landlords who sent harsh rent collectors to squeeze the Irish peasants so mercilessly that most were barely able to subsist.

Making matters worse, because most land holdings were on small plots and were difficult to cultivate efficiently, the English landowners began to consolidate their holdings, remove the Irish peasant from the land, and create pasture where farms once stood. When potato farming became unprofitable for the English landowners, consolidation of small farms increased. The eviction from the land of the Irish peasants became ever more widespread. The many Irish who fled to England were summarily deported by that country, which was itself experiencing harsh economic times and high levels of unemployment. The severest blow to an already fragile Irish economy came in a number of potato famines between 1845 and 1849. Because the potato was a staple of the Irish diet, poor harvests meant at least hardship if not starvation. Successive diseases caused the potato plant to die and the potato to shrivel so as to make it unfit to eat let alone to sell. Between 1846 and 1851, a million Irish died of starvation and disease. As they saw their loved ones die, Irish farmers, once proud of their ability to meet and overcome adversity, finally succumbed to catastrophe and sought relief by emigrating to America.

After 1820, the numbers of Irish immigrants increased rapidly, rising from 54,338 in the decade between 1821 and 1830, to 207,381 between 1831 and 1840. During the two decades between 1841 and 1860, a total of 1,694,838 Irish immigrants came to America. Even during the American Civil War, Irish immigration grew, and between 1861 and 1870, some 435,778 Irish arrived, some of whom had been recruited for service in the Union army. Between 1820 and 1870, about 4,700,000 Irish came to America, a number approximately equal to the entire population of Ireland during the 1970s. Irish immigration declined after 1890.

For the hard-pressed Irish, America was an irresistible lure. For one thing, anti-British feeling lingered in America among people who still remembered the American Revolution and the War of 1812. Many Americans still viewed Irish revolutionaries as patriots not unlike their own Founding Fathers. Since the Irish viewed themselves as a people oppressed by England, just as colonial Americans had been, Irish émigrés thought they would find moral as well as material support from the newly independent Americans as well as from the Irish community already in America. In the United States, farmland was cheap, the demand for labor was insatiable, and the two dollars a day paid for skilled workers and the dollar a day paid for common laborers seemed generous by comparison with wages in Ireland. One unique aspect of Irish immigration during the mid-nineteenth century was the fact that more women than men came to the United States from Ireland. Irish women thought of themselves as self-sufficient and capable of supporting themselves if need be.

Perhaps because of their harsh experiences at home, the Irish peasants who came to America exhibited little interest in the availability of free or cheap land or of planting new roots as farmers. Instead, they became the quintessential urban immigrant and populated the great cities, especially Boston and New York. Like other immigrant groups, the Irish tended to live among people from their own country, thus creating vast ethnic ghettos. In New York, for example, the Irish clustered on the Lower East Side of Manhattan, where they set up Catholic churches and, for the most part, became staunch members of the Democratic Party.

German Immigrants Katharina Dicke, at the age of ninety-two in 1924, could remember her childhood in Württemberg, Germany, where her father had been a shepherd. Her two older sisters and her uncle and aunt had come to the United States first. In 1849 the rest of the family followed. In Fort Wayne, Indiana, Katharina and her sisters worked as maids for English-speaking Americans. A minister from Michigan proposed to her by mail. She accepted and only at the time of her marriage did she first meet her future husband. Two children were born to them in Saginaw, Michigan, and later the family moved to Wisconsin. Katharina Dicke was, at this time, about twenty-five. Of the remaining sixty-seven years of her life she says that although they lived in "circumstances that could be called 'almost poverty,'" she thanks the Lord for all his blessings.[4]

In the 1830s Germany as a nation did not exist. Instead, German-speaking people lived in a number of states of which Prussia and Austria were the most powerful but which included such smaller states as Saxony, Bavaria, and Hannover. The only connection among these states was an agreement not to impose taxes on goods coming from other member states.

By 1848 revolution against the powerful monarchies was sweeping Europe. In the German states it took two forms: continued efforts to unify the many small states into one German nation and the effort to establish a constitutional monarchy, a government in which the monarch would be accountable to an elected legislature. Both efforts failed. Emperor Frederick William IV of Prussia refused to accept limitations on his authority. Unification had to wait for more than twenty years until the Prussian prime minister, Otto von Bismarck, succeeded in uniting the German states into one Germany (without Austria) under Emperor William I. The turmoil that followed these events speeded up German emigration to America.

The period of German emigration roughly paralleled that of the Irish. Through the 1830s the increase in emigration from Germany was gradual, but the numbers rose rapidly during the 1840s and 1850s. Between 1846 and 1855 more than a million Germans came to the United States. Between 1860 and 1890 more immigrants came from Germany than from any other country, and in later decades substantial numbers of Germans continued to arrive.

From eastern and northern Germany came peasants seeking land and the opportunity to restore orthodox Lutheran rituals and traditions in their churches. From southwestern Germany and the Rhineland came political exiles who had participated in the futile Revolution of 1848 to establish parliamentary democracy. The leaders of the revolution were seeking a safe haven. They found one in America. Although not numerous, the political émigrés were generally able men and women who became influential in business and politics and made an important contribution in many fields of endeavor, including business and the arts, government, and politics.

One was Carl Schurz (1829–1906) who, as a student at the University of Bonn, had taken part in the unsuccessful Revolution of 1848. He sought refuge first in France and then, in 1852, in the United States. Schurz worked as a newspaper reporter and became politically active in Wisconsin, an area that was attractive to large numbers of Germans farmers. Schurz supported Lincoln, became a United States minister to Spain, and under President Hayes, served as secretary of the interior. When he died in 1906 he was remembered for insisting upon fairer treatment for the American Indian.

While the Irish were mainly city bound, the Germans were hungry for farmland and tended to settle evenly in the cities and on the farms of the United States. Nevertheless, like the Irish, German immigrants settled in ethnic communities of their own. While the Irish spoke English and could communicate with their neighbors, the Germans established German-speaking enclaves. An area known as Kleindeutchland (Small Germany) contained, until the Civil War, about two-thirds of New York's one hundred thousand Germans. "Here the English language was rarely heard and there was scarcely a business which was not run by Germans. Here also were to be found German churches, schools, restaurants, a Volkstheater, and a lending library."[5] In this area were also the lager beer saloons that were so much at the heart of German immigrant social life. Thus, these "old immigrants" set a pattern and prepared the way for the next wave of immigration, this time from southern and eastern Europe.

Between 1850 and 1882, before the Chinese Exclusion Act of that year closed the gates of immigration against them, 300,000 Chinese came, largely to work on the building of the transatlantic railroads. They were joined by 90,000 Japanese, who were later excluded by the so-called gentlemen's agreement of 1907.

THE NEW IMMIGRANTS
1880–1920

To those immigrants who had arrived decades earlier, it seemed that the new immigrants would never become "American." Their languages were strange, and even the alphabet that some of them used—known as the Cyrillic alphabet—was different. The foods they ate, the clothing they wore, the ways they worshiped, appeared unusually exotic. The new wave of immigrants between 1880 and 1920 triggered a debate as to whether or not the United States should remain committed to the principle of essentially unlimited immigration from Europe and the Western Hemisphere.

Instead of coming from England, Scotland, Wales, Ireland, Germany, and Scandinavia, the new immigrants came from Italy, Russia, the Ukraine, Lithuania, Latvia, Poland, Serbia, Bohemia, Slovakia, Croatia, Hungary, and Greece. They came as well in large numbers from Armenia and Syria. Basques came from Spain and Portugal.

Italian Immigrants Elvira Adorno's father had been in the Italian merchant marine for twenty years, but having decided to come to America, he jumped ship when his ves-

sel docked in New York City. He settled in Little Italy and shortly thereafter sent for his wife and children, including Elvira. In America Elvira's father established his own business, the Adorno Flag Company. He and his wife, a talented embroiderer, lived and worked in a tiny unheated apartment without private toilets. Because of the constant cold, Elvira's mother died and her father was forced to place his children in an orphanage, where Elvira's younger brother died.

Her father decided to remarry so that he could regain custody of his children, but he wanted an Italian wife. His mother in Sicily found a forty-two-year-old seamstress whose passage to America he paid. They were soon married and his children came to live with them. Elvira's father wanted her brothers to become lawyers, but one became an engraver and the other worked for his father in the flag business. Elvira eventually became a teacher in New York City.[6]

While some Italians arrived during the nineteenth century, most came during the first quarter of the twentieth century. In 1907 the number of Italians admitted was greater than the 1960 population of Venice. By 1930 there were more Italians in New York City than in Rome, Italy. A large majority of the Italian immigrants were single men who were willing to do the backbreaking work of constructing railroads, paving streets, cutting stones, and mining coal and other minerals. They also became bootblacks, fruit sellers, shoemakers, barbers, and truck farmers.

Initially many Italian immigrants hoped to put aside a few of their hard-earned dollars and return to Italy, and many, in fact, did so. However, the return to Italy was not without its problems. For one thing, the returned Italian

A Lewis Hine photograph of
newly-arrived immigrants.

immigrant could not readily readjust to the rural Italian environment and to lower wage scales and living standards. As a result, many Italians, after trying to reestablish themselves in the land of their birth, emigrated again to the United States. Moreover, when Italian peasants saw their former neighbors returning looking healthy and prosperous, they too emigrated to America.

Although this was not the only country to which they emigrated, in America Italian peasants saw, or thought they saw, their greatest opportunities for improving their living standard. They fled a land whose rapidly rising population contributed to hunger, disease, homelessness, and poverty. These conditions were aggravated by obsolete methods of farming that made vast tracts of land unproductive. Many still lived in straw houses, rock caves, or one-room shacks, which they shared with their cattle.

In Sicily, the ordinary farm workers earned only eight to thirty-two cents a day; little enough if the workers worked a full year, but the overwhelming majority did not do so. High unemployment, a high birth rate, and malaria and cholera epidemics were among the conditions Italians sought to escape. So dismal were conditions in Italy during those years that some Italian immigrants declared, "We would have eaten each other had we stayed."[7]

To meet the great need for labor in mines and factories, American industrialists imported unskilled labor on a contract basis. The purpose of this practice, made legal by Congress in 1864, was to introduce docile and low paid workers for industrial exploitation. A version of contract labor may be

An espresso shop (coffee shop) was a common sight in Little Italy, the neighborhood in New York City where many Italian immigrants settled.

found in the infamous padrone system by which many Italians were brought to America as unskilled workers.

Labor bosses, or padroni, often recruited children from impoverished rural areas of Italy and transported them, almost like slaves, to the United States, where many were employed as wandering musicians or acrobats. Most of the unskilled adults were hired at fixed wages to work in labor gangs that provided the padrone with a handsome profit. As the number of Italian immigrants grew, the padrone system became unnecessary; nevertheless, the tradition remained, with the padrone now helping the Italian immigrant get a job, send money back home, or otherwise deal with the more frightening aspects of urban life in America. While some padroni did, in this way, still exploit the more helpless people of their country, others provided valuable guidance during a period of difficult adjustment. Because of widespread abuses in the system of importing foreign labor under contract, Congress made the practice illegal in 1885, when it passed the Foran Act.

More than four-fifths of Italian immigrants were clustered in the northeastern part of the United States. New York City had the largest Italian community, followed by Philadelphia, Chicago, Boston, and Newark. While Italians found their way into numerous industries such as shoe factories and textile mills, they largely formed the gangs of pick-and-shovel laborers that helped rebuild the city of Galveston, which was destroyed in the hurricane of 1900 and the city of San Francisco after the 1906 earthquake and fire.

A Jacob Riis photograph of Hester Street, on the Lower East Side of New York City, which was home to many Italian, Slavic, and eastern European Jewish immigrants.

Jewish Immigrants Lizzie Warshavsky's husband, Harry, came to America in the 1880s, then sent for her and married her when she arrived in Saint Louis, Missouri. When the family's financial outlook seemed bleak, Lizzie Warshavsky, a Jewish immigrant from Russia, took matters into her own hands. Harry became nearly blind from his work as a presser in a pants factory and could no longer work, so Lizzie rented a small store, went to a wholesale fabric house, and declared: "I have one hundred and fifty dollars, an empty store, and five mouths to feed. I want three hundred dollars' worth of merchandise."[8] And she got it! On the next visit, she paid the bill and, with another one hundred fifty dollars, got six hundred dollars' worth of merchandise. And Lizzie Warshavsky was in business.

The Jews, next to the Italians, were the most numerous immigrant group to come to America during the late nineteenth and early twentieth centuries. In 1492, when Columbus embarked on his epic journey, Jews were expelled from Spain, a land that had given them sanctuary for centuries. Few could have known that the New World would become the homeland of about one-third of the world's Jews—more Jews than now live in Israel.

In 1654 the first Jews came to the Dutch colony of New Amsterdam and for many years thereafter they remained but a tiny minority in colonial America. In the 1840s German Jews began to arrive in significant numbers, having been uprooted by the political turmoil of those years. While most were poor, some German Jews of this period were members of a kind of Jewish aristocracy who lived lavishly in Fifth Avenue mansions in New York City, or on huge country estates, and enjoyed regular trips to the luxurious resorts of Europe. They established fortunes in retailing (R.H. Macy and Company, Sears Roebuck), finance (Kuhn, Loeb and Company, Lehman Brothers, Goldman, Sachs), mining (Meyer Guggenheim), and grain exporting (Isaac Friedlander).

By 1880, however, the basic character of Jewish immigration began to change as the source of immigration shifted from western Europe (Germany) to eastern Europe (Russia, Poland, Hungary, Romania), where large numbers of Jews had settled. Denied the full privileges of citizenship in most of the countries of eastern Europe, Jews were confined in shtetls, or small villages, in the "pale of settlement," mostly in eastern Poland and western Russia. Jews of eastern Europe had limited access to schools and colleges. Employment in public service, industry, and agriculture was often closed to Jews, and they were denied the opportunity to practice their religion without persecution. Boys from the age of twelve were required to serve in the military. This meant that Jewish boys had to leave their families and were unable to practice their faith, eat kosher food, study the Torah (the Pentateuch), or speak Yiddish, the folk language of their people, as most of them were brought up to do. For these reasons, the Jews of Russia and other eastern European countries sought to leave the lands of their birth.

Pogroms were government-initiated and -inspired episodes of violence against Jewish communities, in which their synagogues, homes, small businesses, and schools were destroyed. After brutal pogroms in 1881–1882, 1891, and 1905–1906, Jewish emigration to America grew rapidly: 5,000 came in 1880; 81,000 in 1892; 258,000 in 1907. Over 2 million Jews left eastern Europe, with 70 percent of these coming from Russia.

The pogroms hastened the flight of the Jews from eastern Europe, and yet, as with other immigrants, the desire to improve their living standard was a vital element in turning the thoughts of eastern European Jews toward America. While some Jews went to Canada, western Europe, Argentina, and—after the establishment of the Zionist movement in 1897—to Palestine, the overwhelming majority came to the United States.

The German Jews, who had come a generation or two earlier, were not particularly pleased to see Jews from eastern Europe coming in such large numbers. They feared that the niche they had carved out for themselves would be eroded and that the extreme orthodoxy of some of these new Jewish immigrants would cast a shadow over their own successful assimilation into the American fabric. Because of their fear of increased anti-Semitism, they initially kept Jews from eastern Europe at arm's length. Yet the numbers were so large, the obligation so unmistakable, and their own self-interest in the welfare of other Jews so undeniable that it was not long before they began to establish organizations to help the new Jewish immigrants adjust to and prosper in America.

THE IMMIGRANT EXPERIENCE

The debate over how many immigrants should be allowed to enter the country, what the criteria for admission ought to be, and how to enforce the admissions criteria is as old as the Republic itself. But while arguments for and against an open immigration policy persisted throughout the nation's history, for the first hundred years there was no federal regulation of the flow of immigration, with the exception of the short-lived and poorly enforced Alien and Sedition and Naturalization Acts of 1798. It was not until almost 1880 that federal laws were passed to restrict immigration.

Until the Civil War, regulation of immigration was undertaken by state governments, particularly those with major ports through which immigrants passed, notably New York, Massachusetts, Pennsylvania, and Maryland. In the case of *City of New York v. Milne* (1837), the Supreme Court upheld the right of states to establish criteria for the admission of immigrants. During the mid-nineteenth century, before Ellis Island became the major point of entry, immigrant arrivals in New York were screened at Castle Garden, a converted concert hall at the southern tip of Manhattan. Commissioners received the immigrants, recorded the name, age, occupation, and religion of each entrant, and noted the value of the belongings that each person brought into the country. Immigrants were given a brief physical examination, and those who were sick were allowed to recuperate after their long journey. Those who were diseased or who in other ways could become a burden on the state were deported. A communal kitchen, an inexpensive restaurant, and employment listings were available to newcomers. An all-volunteer staff offered these immigrants practical tips on getting along in their new environment.

Because skilled and unskilled labor was desperately needed by an expanding nation, many western states sought to pry immigrants loose from their moorings in the port city through which they entered. Some western states even sent brochures overseas offering farmland for as little as $1.25 an acre. In 1845, Michigan sent an agent to the docks of New York to recruit immigrants. Wisconsin also sent agents to New York but went a step further and compiled mailing lists of relatives of immigrants still in Europe, encouraging them to come to that state. Minnesota sent advertisements in English, Welsh, German, Dutch, Norwegian, and Swedish. It offered prizes for the best essay describing the opportunities for the immigrant in Minnesota. And a pamphlet from Minnesota declared, "It is well to exchange the tyrannies and thankless toil of the old world for the freedom and independence of the new."[9]

These efforts by the states were supplemented by promotions made by the railroads, which encouraged immigrants to travel by train to the western states. Railroads also had vast tracts of land to sell and wooed immigrants as potential purchasers. The Illinois Central, for example, as early as 1854 sent agents to the German states and to the

Women working on engine parts at a Ford Motor Company plant in Michigan in 1914. Many immigrant women were employed in the growing industries of the United States.

Scandinavian countries. These agents offered various inducements in the form of discounted railroad tickets and even help with the costs of the journey overseas by ship.

While immigrants today come mostly by plane, in the nineteenth century they came by ship. During the first half of that century those ships were still largely sailing vessels, and if the immigrants were lucky and the weather fair, the journey took about forty-four days, although journeys of eight weeks were not uncommon. Travel under sail was never comfortable, since the ships were built to carry cargo rather than passengers. Later immigrants, however, endured worse conditions. They traveled in the overcrowded, poorly ventilated steerage section of the ship where they slept and ate and lived like the livestock they often carried with them. Because there was not enough food to go around, hunger and even starvation were common. With inadequate toilet facilities, cholera, dysentery, and typhoid were rampant on some vessels. Helpless passengers often had to protect themselves from some fellow travelers who were prostitutes and thieves, as well as vicious crewmen who sometimes beat them.

By 1882, forty-eight steamship companies offered transportation across the Atlantic. Competition for passengers was sharp between the older Cunard and Hamburg-Amerika lines and the newer Holland-America, White Star, Red Star, and numerous others. One could go from England to the United states for 12 to 15 dollars. It cost 30 dollars to go from Copenhagen, Denmark, to New York. From Odessa, Russia, to the Dakota territory one had to have the princely sum of 75 dollars. In many cases, children were allowed to travel free with one or both parents. New arrivals often received prepaid boat tickets from relatives and friends who had arrived earlier. Some historians estimate that up to 70 percent of voyagers in the middle to latter part of the nineteenth century used prepaid tickets.

The journey across the ocean by steamship in 1867 took about fourteen days; by 1897 it took only about eight days. Passengers had their own berths, men and women slept separately, and the ship was required to make three meals a day available. Overcrowding, however, was still the rule and in rough seas the travelers must have wondered if the journey was really worth it.

In an attempt to ease the transition of "greenhorns," as they were called, immigrant-aid societies proliferated. These groups were organized not so much to promote immigration, as to care for the immigrants. The societies provided interpreters, offered help in finding clean, respectable rooms in boardinghouses, sought job opportunities for the newcomers, or offered them guidance on securing employment.

THE GOLDEN DOOR:
IMMIGRANT EXPECTATIONS

"The golden door" is a term coined by Emma Lazarus, whose words are inscribed on the base of the Statue of Liberty in New York Harbor: "Give me your tired, your poor; /Your huddled masses, yearning to breathe free . . . /Send these, the homeless, tempest-tossed to me: I lift my lamp beside the golden door." The "golden door" is a metaphor for the largest port of entry, New York. It can also suggest the high expectations immigrants have for their future in America.

Most immigrants discovered America by reading the letters home of family and friends. Although a few had literally expected to find streets paved with gold, as the advertising of transportation companies often implied, most immigrants had more reasonable expectations.

In our day of instantaneous global communication, of telephones, faxes, and television, a letter from America may not be so significant. But for most of the nineteenth and early twentieth century, a letter from America generated more excitement in the family to which it was addressed, and in the village in which the family lived, than one would now readily believe. The letter from America was "borne in triumph and opened with joy."[10] Immigrants wrote about their work, the soil, their experiences as carpenters, farmers, bricklayers, or housemaids. They wrote about their lives in windowless tenements and about their work in the dark of a mine shaft or in miserable factories known as sweatshops, where they made clothing or rolled cigars.

A section of Chicago, circa 1906, to which many immigrants from Slavic countries moved.

Harsh though their lives often were, their letters for the most part praised the new land. They usually told of higher wages, of jobs more readily available, of land more easily acquired and cultivated than in the old country. The letters described the richer opportunities and greater personal and religious freedom the newcomers had found. In 1845, a group of Norwegian immigrants wrote: "We have no expectation of gaining riches, but we live under a liberal government in a fruitful land, where freedom and equality are the rule in religious and civil matters, and where each of us is at liberty to earn his living practically as he chooses. Such opportunities are more to be desired than riches."[11]

The first step in "making it" in America was to find a job. Depending upon one's skills and the economic circumstances at the time, that task was more daunting for some than it was for others.

Those who came to America expecting quick riches were doomed to disappointment. In Sweden farmworkers earned $33.50 a year plus room and board. Little wonder that a salary of $40 a month in a coal mine, or $200 dollars a year as a farmhand, was appealing. These figures by themselves do not tell of the harsh desolation of the often storm-swept plains of Kansas, Nebraska, Minnesota, and the Dakotas. They do not tell of the squalid conditions in factories where immigrants worked and slums in which they lived, nor do they speak of the labor unions that resented the newcomers' presence and often refused them membership. But despite the hardships, most immigrants succeeded in America, obtaining decent wages and occupations.

How does one explain such success? It takes hard work, grit, initiative, imagination, and creativity, which most immigrants had. One must remember that immigrants are a very special group. It requires a great deal of courage to leave one's native land and move to an unfamiliar place. Those qualities of mind and body, which sustain the immigrants in the search for opportunity also sustain them in the new land.

At various times America has been called a melting pot, a mosaic, and a kaleidoscope.

MELTING POT

In 1908 the English dramatist Israel Zangwill wrote a play about the marriage of a Russian-born Jew and a Russian-born Christian. The play, entitled *The Melting Pot*, was a huge success in New York City. The title became a sort of shorthand for the process that occurs to the newcomer to America. In the words of Zangwill's hero: "There she lies, the great Melting Pot—listen! . . . Yes, east and west, north and south, the palm and the pine, the pole and the equator, the Crescent and the Cross—how the great alchemist melts and fuses them with his purging flame! Here shall they all unite to build the republic of Man and the Kingdom of God . . . What is the glory of Rome and Jerusalem, where all nations and races come to worship and look back, compared with the glory of America, where all nations come to harbor and look forward."[12]

The idea of America as a melting pot was vaguely understood long before it was articulated. A melting pot, literally, is a vessel into which a number of metals are melted down and fused into a new substance. Zangwill believed that the essential experience of the immigrant was that of shedding his or her native language and customs and emerging as a new person, an American.

The melting pot metaphor was implicit in the words of Michel Guillaume Jean de Crèvecoeur (1735–1813) who wrote in the early eighteenth century, "Here individuals of all nations are melted into a new race of men." And Ralph Waldo Emerson (1803–1882), writing in the mid-ninteenth century, declared that the American "is the most composite of all creatures . . . the Irish, Germans, Swedes, Poles, and Cossacks, and all the European tribes—of the Africans, and Polynesians—will construct a new race, a new religion, a new state, a new literature, which will be as vigorous as the new Europe which came out of the smelting pot of the Dark Ages."

The distinguished historian Frederick Jackson Turner (1861–1932) was convinced that it was the frontier that Americanized, liberated, and fused the immigrants into a new race that was English neither in nationality nor in characteristics. And President Theodore Roosevelt, who deplored "hyphenated Americans"—that is, those who described themselves as German-American or Irish-American—insisted that, "We Americans are the children of the crucible." When Israel Zangwill dedicated his play to him, Theodore Roosevelt could not have been more pleased.

Herman Melville (1819–1891), the American author of one of the world's great novels, *Moby Dick*, wrote: "Our blood is as the blood of the Amazon, made up of a thousand noble currents all pouring into one. We are not a nation so much as a world."

The "melting pot" idea held the imagination of Americans and offered the hope and expectation that the new immigrants, however strange they may appear at first would, in due course, become assimilated into the general population. Moreover, unlike the practice in most countries, in the United States immigrants could readily become American citizens and the overwhelming majority did so. So great was the conviction among the masses of the people that immigrants would fuse into the American mainstream, that the Zangwill play, which reinforced the "melting pot" concept, may have delayed for at least a decade legislation restricting immigration. Well up to the outbreak of World War II, even though new immigration had been reduced to a trickle, America as a "melting pot" was a widely held concept.

As a more sophisticated view of what actually happened to the immigrant took root, however, it became clearer that the "melting pot" concept was flawed in that it had racist overtones suggesting that what the immigrants brought here from their native lands was somehow inferior to whatever it was that was American. The melting pot concept implied that there was something shameful in the origins, habits, language, religion, and attitudes of the mainly southern and eastern Europeans which was best obliterated. It further assumed that eventually all immigrants would be washed with the American bleach and would emerge purer and better, uniform in speech, manner, outlook, and values.

MOSAIC

Zangwill was wrong; the immigrants refused to melt. It is true, of course, that they did not remain unalterably German or Irish, Swedish or Polish; they also never gave up entirely their roots and traditions. Protected as they were by the Constitution and the Bill of Rights, they could practice their religion freely, and establish newspapers and magazines in their own languages. They could not be compelled to master English; some never did.

The American as a new and different person never really emerged, as even a superficial examination of what actually happened to old and new immigrants alike will verify. Rather than "melting pot," the concept of cultural pluralism or cultural mosaic may be a far better description of immigrant experiences in America.

If the melting pot concept is derived from engineering or metallurgy, the mosaic concept is derived from art. A mosaic is a picture or decoration made of bits of inlaid stone, glass, or jewels, often held in place by a lead border. In this concept, America is viewed as an artistic and carefully balanced construction, with people from many nations retaining some of their customs, languages, and traditions while pulling together for America. While the immigrants did not remain unchanged, they added to the mosaic of America as a nation of many nationalities, religions, and races. "E Pluribus Unum," the national maxim, which is Latin for "one out of many," still expresses the distinctive American ability to reconcile unity with diversity.

KALEIDOSCOPE

Each successive wave of immigrants gave America a distinctive cast for a time: then as the earlier immigrants become an increasingly important part of the nation's mainstream, the nation was again changed. Laurence Fuchs[13] uses the term "kaleidoscope," a reference to the optical device in which designs are in constant motion and ever changing. When in 1965, the United States once again opened the doors to immigration, the patterns in that kaleidoscope began to change rapidly.

By the 1870s some 280,000 immigrants were arriving each year at American ports. With a volume so large, the federal government could no longer remain aloof; some national approach to immigration was needed. In 1875 the U.S. Supreme Court reversed itself and in the case of *Henderson v. Mayor of New York* declared that existing state immigration laws were unconstitutional in that they were contrary to the exclusive power of Congress to regulate foreign commerce. "It is equally clear," the justices continued, "that the matter of these statutes may be, and ought to be, the subject of a uniform system or plan. . . . We are of the opinion that this whole subject has been confided to Congress by the Constitution; and that Congress can more appropriately and with more acceptance exercise it than any other body known to our law, state or nation; that by providing a system of laws in these matters, applicable to all ports, to all vessels, a serious question, which has long been a matter of contest and complaint, may be effectively and satisfactorily settled."

Thus the federal government assumed responsibility for the flow of immigrants from abroad. With that power went the authority to keep the door to immigration wide open or to reduce the flow of immigrants to a trickle. Federal policy toward immigration was erratic and fickle. There was, at first, a desire for welcoming the immigrant in the hundred year tradition of the nation. But there was also a knee-jerk reaction to exclude, in response to real or imagined fears of what strangers may do to the character and economy of America. Thus, American immigration policy has wavered between a tendency to welcome and a tendency to exclude.

CHAPTER THREE

THE CLOSING DOOR
1920–1965

FINAL ARRANGEMENTS FOR DISEMBARKATION
of all passengers complete. Governments of
Belgium, Holland, France, and England, co-
operated magnificently with American Joint
Distribution committee to effect this possibility.

—The Voyage of the Damned[1]

The restrictiveness of American immigration in the
mid-twentieth century can be seen in the tragic saga of a
shipload of 937 mostly Jewish passengers who were
allowed to leave Nazi Germany in 1939 for Cuba, which
had agreed to accept them. When the ship arrived, however, Cuban officials refused it entry and the vessel, the
St. Louis of the Hamburg-America Line, was forced to sail
the seas for weeks, sometimes within twenty miles of
Miami, Florida, because no nation would accept its passengers. When the vessel's captain was ordered to return
to Nazi Germany, the crematoria of the concentration camps
seemed to be the passengers' tragic destiny. However, in
a last-minute reversal, several nations grudgingly agreed
to accept a portion of them. The United States was not
among them.

In 1776 Thomas Paine (1737–1809), whose writings
helped to prepare the way for the American Revolution,
declared that the new nation would become "An asylum
for mankind." A poll undertaken by *Fortune* magazine in

1939 asked Americans this question: "If you were a member of Congress would you vote yes or no on a bill to open the doors of the United States to a larger number of refugees than are now admitted under our immigration quotas?" Of those responding, 83 percent replied no. The message was clear: refugees were not welcome.[2] Why had Americans changed their minds?

RESTRICTING IMMIGRATION
1789–1865

In the early eighteenth century Benjamin Franklin worried about the number of German immigrants coming to America. That quintessential American, the oldest framer of the Constitution, observed that German immigrants "are generally the most stupid of their own nation . . . it is almost impossible to remove any prejudices they entertain." Even Thomas Jefferson, author of the Declaration of Independence and third president of the United States, was concerned that immigrants would not "harmonize" with those already here. In his view immigrants would "bring with them the principles of government they leave . . . or if they throw them off, it will be in exchange for unbounded licentiousness. . . . These principles, with their language, they will transmit to their children."

Before the Civil War, religious prejudice interfered with the development of a wise immigration policy. The first targets of persecution were the Irish, whose Catholic religion and adherence to papal doctrine seemed to clash with Protestant belief. The warning "No Irish need apply" commonly accompanied job advertisements in an age when antidiscrimination legislation had not yet been contemplated.

Samuel F. B. Morse (1791–1872), who later invented the telegraph, was particularly alarmed. In 1834, he urged Americans to protect themselves from a Roman Catholic conspiracy. "To your post!" he cried. "Fly to protect the vulnerable places of your Constitution and Laws. Place your guards; you will need them, and quickly too. And first, shut your gates."[3]

Nor was Morse alone in his alarm. The distinguished preacher and abolitionist Lyman Beecher (1775–1863) was so concerned about the rapid increase in the number of Roman Catholics coming to America, and the growth in the size and number of Catholic churches, that he became convinced there was a conspiracy by the papacy to take over the young country. When Catholics in New York and elsewhere objected to the use in schools of the Protestant King James Bible and sought funds for their own schools, the hostility of the Protestants grew.

Antagonism toward Catholics, Jews, and foreigners sometimes causes nativism. Nativists believe that those born in America are superior to immigrants, who bring their strange customs, speak English haltingly, and worship in other than mainstream Protestant churches. Nativist ideas formed the main thrust of a secret organization called the Know-Nothings, whose name came from their response,"—I know nothing"—to queries about their views and plans.

This nativist group, which was anti-Catholic, anti-foreigner, anti-immigrant, became strong enough to form the American Party, which in 1854 won control of several state governments and sent a number of representatives to Congress. In 1856, some members of Congress complained that European nations were making America a "receptacle for the dregs and offscourings of their population." And in the same year a congressional committee expressed its fear that too many immigrants were paupers and criminals and that "A nation of freemen, no matter how great and powerful, cannot long continue as such without religion and morality, industry and frugality."[4]

Despite its minor victories, the Know-Nothings never secured the enactment of legislation limiting the number of immigrants to America. The debate did not end, however. Instead, the fear of foreigners was shunted aside by concern over slavery, the Civil War, and the reconstruction of a war-weary nation.

THE GATES BEGIN TO CLOSE
1865–1917

In 1849 gold was discovered at a sawmill being built for John Sutter, an early settler in California. The gold rush that followed propelled that territory to early statehood in 1850. To the tune of Stephen Foster's "Oh! Susanna," a multitude of adventurers journeyed west and risked everything in the attempt to strike it rich. Because of the vast and rapid population buildup in California, Congress offered generous grants and made cheap land available to the Union Pacific Railroad to lay tracks from Omaha, Nebraska, west to California, and to the Central Pacific to expand its route eastward from Sacramento, California. The "wedding of the rails" was celebrated in Ogden, Utah, in 1865 when two locomotives "kissed."

Among those observing these festivities were some of the many Irish immigrants who had provided the muscle for the laying of rails for the Union Pacific. Also watching were some of the ten thousand unskilled Chinese laborers known as coolies, who had been hired by the Central Pacific. The Chinese were considered cheap, efficient, and docile workers. By the time the golden spike uniting the Union and Central Pacific railroads was driven into the ground in Utah, some 63,000 Chinese had come to the United States. Twice that number would come in the next decade. Even before this rapid buildup of Chinese immigrants, cries were heard to curb their immigration. In

response to demands of congressional representatives in western states, who were being pressured by labor unions who feared that Chinese laborers would work for low pay, Congress sought ways to exclude the Chinese.

In the Burlingame Treaty (1868) between the United States and China, the United States had pledged not to restrict the number of Chinese immigrants coming into the country. This concession had been made in exchange for trade privileges in China. In 1879, despite the terms of the Burlingame Treaty, Congress passed legislation limiting Chinese immigration. The proposal was vetoed by President Rutherford B. Hayes (1877–1881), however, because he felt it to be contrary to the agreement. Nevertheless, a year later a new treaty was negotiated, giving the United States the right to "regulate, limit, or suspend," but not absolutely prohibit, the immigration of Chinese laborers. This gave Congress a loophole, and in 1882 it passed the Chinese Exclusion Act, which suspended Chinese immigration for ten years and barred Chinese immigrants from becoming citizens. The immigration act of 1882 barred the entry of "lunatics, idiots, convicts, and those liable to become public charges." The latter provision would be invoked again and again to keep out those seeking political asylum. Thus a precedent was established. If one group of immigrants could be excluded, why not others? What had been done once could and would be done again.

Despite the dedication of the Statue of Liberty in 1886 and Emma Lazarus's welcome to the "huddled masses," Congress gradually sought to exclude various classes of immigrants. In 1891 Congress denied entry to paupers,

A Chinese young man seeking to enter the United States is questioned closely by the authorities.

polygamists (those who have more than one wife), and persons suffering from contagious diseases. When President William McKinley was shot in 1901 by a foreign anarchist, anti-foreign sentiment mounted. Congress again responded in 1903 by barring anarchists who believed in the forceful overthrow of government or in assassination of public officials. It also excluded prostitutes, beggars, and epileptics. In 1907, imbeciles, tuberculosis sufferers, and those accused of a morally shameful crime were excluded. In the same year, according to the terms of a gentlemen's agreement between Japan and the United States, Japan agreed to limit the number of its people who could emigrate to America.

In 1894, the Boston-based Immigration Restriction League urged that Congress pass a measure requiring that all new immigrants be literate. In the words of the poet Thomas Bailey Aldrich, this group sought legislation against "accents of menace alien to our air." Legislation to this effect was introduced thirty-two times but was either defeated in Congress or vetoed by the president.

In 1907, at the request of President Theodore Roosevelt (1901–1909) Congress established an Immigration Commission, chaired by Senator William P. Dillingham, a Republican from Vermont. In 1911, after a three-year study, the expenditure of over a million dollars, and the utilization of a staff of three hundred, the Dillingham Commission issued a massive forty-one-volume report. The report emphasized that the new immigrants were "inferior" to those who had come in earlier years in that they did not assimilate well and their presence caused a decrease in wages and job opportunities for Americans. The report,

In the period following World War I
the welcoming light grew dim.

like most such reports, was a mixture of nativist and economic arguments against further rapid increases in immigration, and it laid the foundation for comprehensive immigration legislation.

In 1917, partly because of the impact of the Dillingham Commission's report, Congress imposed a literacy test for immigrants. The legislation, adopted over the veto of President Woodrow Wilson (1913–1921), provided that no alien over sixteen years of age who could not read some language or dialect would be admitted to the United States. Also excluded by this legislation were alcoholics, vagrants, and persons with mental difficulties. Asians not already barred by the Chinese Exclusion Act or the gentlemen's agreement were likewise excluded. The 1917 legislation, the most comprehensive immigration measure up to that time, increased the tax immigrants had to pay to eight dollars. The head tax, as it was called, clearly signaled that America had turned the corner from welcome for all to restriction and even exclusion.

THE LAMP BESIDE THE GOLDEN DOOR DIMS 1920–1965

The turmoil of World War I (1914–1918) stopped immigration for a time. But during the early 1920s immigration resumed. In 1921, for example, 800,000 new immigrants were recorded. This time, however, America was far from welcoming. As the boys came marching home at the end of World War I, the fanfare and celebration attending their return expressed the nation's relief that the Great War was over, but it could not hide the nation's disillusionment over the war's results—the numbers of dead and the political outcome. As America began to withdraw from involvement in foreign affairs into the storm cellar of neutrality, a parallel development was the relatively abrupt closing of the door to immigration.

The Ku Klux Klan marches in Binghamton, New York, in the 1920s. The Klan portrayed immigrants who were not Anglo-Saxon and Protestant as a danger to America.

Fear of Communist infiltration into American life, sometimes called the "red scare," was likewise a characteristic of the early post-World War I years. Nativism was again on the rise and the Ku Klux Klan not only terrorized American blacks but also fanned the flames of religious and racial hatred. Anti-Semitism was rampant, and there was fear of the so-called international Jew. Henry Ford's newspaper, the *Dearborn Independent*, spread lies about a dangerous international Jewish conspiracy. Jews were denied jobs on the basis of their religion, and numerous hotels and country clubs excluded Jews.

Some races, according to the theories of the day, were

deemed inferior because of alleged genetic physical or mental flaws. Even reformers despaired of "reforming" the newcomers. They were looked upon as people who would never learn to use soap, keep their homes clean, speak English, or otherwise improve themselves, to say nothing about improving their adopted land. Every time reformers seemed to be improving life in the urban slums, a new immigrant group would flood the area and destroy what had been achieved.

Labor feared that the immigrants would work for lower wages and take their jobs. In 1890 the census had declared that the frontier was closed, so where would the new immigrants find land? How would they support themselves and their families? Would they become dependent upon established Americans?

Americans too, were disappointed with the fruits of their involvement in World War I and took a dim view of foreign people and goods. During these years, America sought to minimize its exposure to international affairs by adopting a policy of isolation. It is no coincidence, perhaps, that just as it raised its tariff barriers against goods coming from other countries, it also raised the barriers against people seeking refuge in America.

Against this background Congress resumed the debate about whether or not America should remain a land of refuge for immigrants. The new immigrants were largely, but not exclusively, Catholic (Italian) and Jewish (eastern European), and both groups were the targets of bigotry. Congress sought to pass legislation that would encourage the flow of immigrants from northern and western Europe at the expense of those from southern and eastern Europe. When it became clear that the literacy tests for immigration would not restrict the numbers of immigrants from Southern and Eastern Europe, Congress passed more restrictive legislation in 1921 and again in 1924.

The Immigration Act of 1921 limited immigration to an

annual 3 percent of the number of foreign born of each nationality based on the census of 1910. A maximum quota was 357,000. However, at that time the United States sought to maintain good diplomatic relations with Latin America, and because cheap labor from Mexico was needed on the farms of California and the Southwest, no limits were placed on immigration from countries of the Western Hemisphere.

Within quota limits, the Immigration Act of 1921 gave preference to citizens' "wives, parents, brothers, sisters, or children under eighteen years of age." Establishing priorities based on family relationships represented a new approach to immigration policy. Another new element in the law was the establishment of a nonquota category, which gave preference to actors, artists, lecturers, singers, nurses, ministers, and professors. Later, wives and dependent children of U.S. citizens were allowed to enter over and above a nation's quota. In this departure, nonquota immigrants were admitted on the basis of the kind of person they were rather than the country from which they came. While immigration laws would change greatly in the 1960s, immigration guidelines that encourage family unity remain an important element in American immigration policy.

The Immigration Act of 1924, sometimes called the Johnson-Reed Act, was even more drastic. That law reduced the number of immigrants who could come to America to 165,000 and the annual quota for each nation was set at 2 percent of those who had come in 1890. The application of the census of 1890 rather than the 1910 census gave additional preference to immigrants from northern and western Europe.

The 1924 legislation was fine-tuned by the National Origins Act of 1929. This law limited immigration to an annual total of just over 150,000 that would be based on national origins. Instead of having a fixed quota for each nation, there would be a quota for each nationality in proportion to its percentage of the general population of the nation in 1920. A minimum quota for any nationality was 100. Restrictions on Asians were reaffirmed. All immigrants had to obtain a visa from an American consul in the country from which they sought to emigrate. This made it possible for immigration authorities to screen potential immigrants. For over thirty-five years, between 1929 and 1965, this was the immigration policy of the United States.

The 1920s legislation based U.S. policy on blatantly nativist views and religious, racial, and ethnic bigotry. The intent of the legislation was not merely to limit the number of immigrants entering the country but to preserve the basic racial composition of the nation. Senator Albert Johnson, the chief sponsor of the legislation, boasted that the myth of the melting pot had been discredited and that "The United States is our land. If it was not the land of our fathers, at least it may be, and it should be, the land of our children. We intend to maintain it so. The day of unalloyed welcome to all peoples, the day of indiscriminate acceptance of all races, has definitely ended."[5]

Soon after the restrictive immigration legislation with its emphasis on the ethnicity was passed, Adolf Hitler came to power in Germany and built a nation, indeed an empire, on false notions of racial superiority and religious bigotry not unlike those that served as the philosophical underpinnings of the immigration laws of the 1920s.

The high tariff policy of the 1920s contributed to economic stagnation and worldwide depression, which were among the causes of World War II. American isolationism, of which the restrictive immigration legislation of the 1920s was a part, reduced the American voice in global affairs. In 1939, World War II broke out, and two years later America was drawn into a conflict it had not done very much to prevent. When a shortsighted Congress passed restrictions on the immigration of the "yellow peril," anti-

American sentiment flared in Japan. This played into the hands of the Japanese militarists, who began the conquest of Asia that ended in the attack on Pearl Harbor.

THE AFTERMATH OF
IMMIGRATION RESTRICTION

In October of 1929, the American stock market crashed, heralding the onset of a global depression that did not end until the world's resources were drawn upon to wage the Second World War. In those circumstances emigration to America would have slowed very substantially even without the restrictionist policy America had adopted.

As the depression deepened, President Herbert Hoover (1929–1933) ordered more rigorous enforcement of the provision barring those from entering the country who were "liable to become public charges." Consequently, only the reasonably prosperous could enter. During these years of economic hardship, many who would have preferred to leave the country in which they were born did not have the financial means to do so. Moreover, because of the depression, America's image as a land of economic opportunity was diminished. As a result, many quotas remained unfilled and, in some years, more people left this country than entered it.

The most baneful, if unintended, consequence of immigration restriction of the depression years was that it made entry of refugees from Hitler's Germany extremely difficult and only a small fraction of those deserving political asylum received it. Throughout the 1930s, Congress adamantly refused to liberalize quota restrictions even when quotas were unfilled. When Senator Robert Wagner of New York and Representative Edith Rogers of Massachusetts sought to get congressional approval for the rescue of 10,000 refugee children under the age of fourteen, in 1939 and 1940, the measure was defeated. The unwillingness of the nation to open its doors to Jewish and other refugees from Hitler's Europe has been described as the "worst failure" of Franklin D. Roosevelt.[6]

The restrictive immigration laws of the 1920s led to a decline in immigration from Europe and the beginning of an increase of immigrants from other areas that were not subject to quota limitations. Between 1924 and 1934, the Philippine Islands was the only Pacific nation whose inhabitants had not been excluded. By 1920 only 5,000 Filipinos were living on the U.S. mainland. By 1930, however, ten times that many Filipinos had entered, and once again demands were made by labor unions and others that the doors of immigration be slammed against them. When in 1935 the Philippine Islands became an American commonwealth as an interim step toward independence, an annual quota of 50 persons was allotted. When on July 4, 1946, the Philippines became independent, Filipinos were completely excluded despite their heroic role in World War II.

In 1942, when America needed the labor of aliens to help it with its war effort, the bracero program, which allowed Mexicans to work temporarily in America's industries, was adopted. And because of the U.S. wartime alliance with China, the ban on Chinese immigrants was repealed. In 1946 the War Brides Act was adopted by Congress, allowing 120,000 spouses and children of those who had served in the American armed services to immigrate to the United States.

It was not until the war's end that Congress grudgingly adopted the Displaced Persons Acts of 1948 and 1950, which allowed the admission of 415,744 refugees. By June of 1952 most of those who were displaced by the turmoil of World War II had been resettled, most of them in America. But by then refugees from Hitler were not the only ones in need of political refuge. Between 1953 and 1957 Congress adopted legislation allowing some refugees from Communist dominated countries to come to the United

States. These were merely exceptions to the national policy of curtailing immigration; there was no change in policy. Indeed, the exceptions were counted against future quota allocations.

That America had hardened its heart against immigrants was reaffirmed in the McCarran-Walter Immigration and Nationality Act of 1952, which Congress adopted over the veto of President Harry Truman. This legislation changed the formula for computing the annual quota of each country to one-sixth of one percent of the number of persons of that particular national origin who were in the United States in 1920. In effect, McCarran-Walter simplified the application of the racist national origins quotas of earlier legislation.

Excessively harsh provisions were aimed at those even suspected of having Communist sympathies. Under McCarran-Walter, western Europe received 85 percent of the total annual number. Moreover, immigrants from colonies of European nations could no longer enter under the quotas assigned to the colonial power. This provision was aimed at cutting down the number of black immigrants who came from the British West Indies under the generous British quota.

Among the liberal features of McCarran-Walter were the elimination of the category of aliens ineligible for citizenship, a modest expansion of quotas from China and Japan, and the establishment of token quotas for other countries in the Asia-Pacific area. Special preference categories were set up for immigrants with advanced education, technical skills, or other desirable abilities. The nonquota class of immigrants was expanded to encourage the entry of immediate relatives of citizens and permanent-resident aliens. Thousands of spouses were able to join their husbands or wives in the United States.

Despite these liberalizing provisions, President Truman found the law objectionable. In vetoing the legislation he declared: "The basis of this quota system was false and unworthy in 1924. It is even worse now . . . this quota system keeps out the very people we want to bring in. It is incredible to me that . . . we should again be enacting into law such a slur on the patriotism, the capacity, and the decency of a large part of our citizenry."[7]

McCarran-Walter reflected the paranoia of the nation on the subject of immigration. On the one hand there was fear that subversives from Communist countries were about to inundate the United States. On the other hand there was an awareness that not all of those with different views ought to be excluded from entering the country. Nativism retained a grip on the America, but there was a growing sensitivity that just as the civil rights movement was gaining momentum at home, the human rights of those seeking to improve their lives by entering the country could not be violated. Although Congress passed McCarran-Walter over President Truman's veto, the President, at least, understood that a racist approach to immigration could not be sustained.

IMMIGRATION RESUMES
1965–1994

AMERICANS GO TO BANK FOR LOAN, Vietnamese go to friends. I ask this guy for a thousand, another for two thousand, soon I have eighteen thousand. We trust each other, so no interest. He know I do the same for him one day." In 1985, Gi opened his computer store. "At first I keep old job while wife and friend take care of store; later I quit to run business full time. Until last year we are here seven days a week sometimes until two in the morning. Now we're doing okay. We take Sundays off.

—Nguyen Hu Gi, who opened
his computer store in Little
Saigon, a community of 70,000
Vietnamese, the largest outside
of Vietnam itself, located just
south of Los Angeles[1]

The 1984 Olympic Games were opened by Thomas Bradley, the mayor of Los Angeles and a descendant of African slaves. In the Olympic march of the nations, the United States was represented by American Indians. In the stadium, Chinese-Americans cheered for the athletes from the People's Republic of China. Irish-Americans, Italian-Americans, Korean-Americans, "and at least forty other ethnic groups rooted for the teams from their ancestral homelands as well as for Americans. Buddhists, Sikhs, Taoists, and Hindus—no less American than their blue-eyed and blond neighbors—cheered the victories of American athletes."[2]

After over forty years of pursuing a policy that essentially closed off immigration, the United States in 1965 had reopened the doors to immigrants.

AMERICA FLINGS OPEN
ITS DOORS

In May of 1954, in *Brown v. the Board of Education of Topeka, Kansas*, the Supreme Court concluded that "in the field of public education, the doctrine of 'separate but equal' has no place." With this decision the tortuous process to end discrimination in schools began. On December 1, 1955, forty-two-year-old Rosa Parks, a seamstress in Montgomery, Alabama, refused to give up her seat on a crowded bus to a white man. She had been sitting between the "white only" part of the bus and the area reserved for "colored." Ms. Parks believed she was breaking no law. Nevertheless, the driver stopped the bus and called the police. Rosa Parks was arrested and taken to jail.

The Montgomery bus boycott that followed this incident ended successfully when, in November 1956, the Montgomery federal court struck down city and state segregation laws, a decision that was upheld by the U.S. Supreme Court. Thus was launched the campaign of the 1960s to end racial segregation and to achieve human rights for all Americans. The Civil Rights Act of 1964, the Voting Rights Act of 1965, and the Immigration and Nationality (Hart-Celler) Act of the same year were among the fruits of these efforts.

The 1952 McCarran-Walter Act was clearly at odds with a nation whose attitudes toward race and ethnicity were being forced to change. If overt racism was intolerable at home, was it not also intolerable to use racism as a measure of the worth of those wishing to enter the United States as immigrants? Were the racist fallacies upon which the 1952 immigration bill was based appropriate for a nation that believed itself to be the leader of the free world? President John F. Kennedy attacked the McCarran-Walter Act and charged that it had no "basis in either logic or reason. It neither satisfies a national need nor accomplishes an international purpose."[3]

The Hart-Celler legislation of 1965 had been supported by President John F. Kennedy but was passed after his death with the support of his brother, Senator Edward Kennedy, and his successor as President, Lyndon Johnson. The new legislation swept away the quotas based on national origin, a principle dedicated to the impossible ideal that the ethnic composition of America should be approximately what it was in 1920.

This was the first time that the countries of the Western Hemisphere had been assigned a numerical ceiling. Family reunification, which accounted for about 74 percent of the total, not ethnic origin, was to be the major measure by which immigrants were to be chosen and applicants were to be admitted on a first-come, first-served basis. The law set up preference categories, with those in the highest preference category given the highest priority, or the first opportunity to enter the United States.

The preference classes established the following order of priority:

1. Unmarried adult sons and daughters of U.S. citizens (20 percent)
2. Spouses and unmarried sons and daughters of resident aliens (20 percent of total plus any unused portion of class number 1)
3. Members of the professions, including doctors,

lawyers, teachers, and others with special talents or education (10 percent)

4. Married sons and daughters of U.S. citizens (10 percent of total plus the unused portion of classes 1, 2, and 3)

5. Brothers and sisters of U.S. citizens (24 percent of the total plus any unused portion of classes 1 to 4)

6. Skilled and unskilled persons to fill specified labor needs in the United States (10 percent)

7. Refugees from Communist, or Communist-dominated, areas and from the Middle East and persons made homeless by natural calamity (6 percent)

Three categories of exclusions were also established:

1. Those with mental disease, drug addiction, or alcohol addiction

2. Criminals, prostitutes, and those with contagious diseases

3. Subversives—that is, those whose past record indicated that they might try to undermine the U.S. government

In 1980 refugees were eliminated as a preferential category. A worldwide ceiling on immigration of 270,000 (down from 290,000) was set, although refugees were no longer counted in the quota. Moreover, refugees could come from countries other than those dominated by Communists and those in the Middle East.

Under the family unification policy,
Nicola Fuccilli brought his wife
and eleven children from Italy
to the United States in 1963.

THE NEWEST IMMIGRANTS
1965–1995

Under the new legislation, 86 percent of the newest immigrants come from Latin America (45 percent) and Asia (41 percent), while Europe contributes only 10 percent. Whereas most immigrants from Europe were once traditionally male, white, and single, a majority of the newest immigrants are women, many are people of color, and many more are married. Although most of today's newcomers come from Third World countries—poor nations whose economies are still developing—many of the newest immigrants are professionally trained (engineers, for example, or computer technicians) or have managerial skills. The profiles of these new immigrants portend enormous changes in America's lifestyles; its tastes in food, clothing, and entertainment; its racial and religious composition; and even its language.

The newest wave of immigration, like the earlier ones, has triggered resentment among those Americans whose roots were planted here generations ago. Will the new immigrants learn English, some people wonder? Will they be a burden on the taxpayer who will be forced to care for the poor among them? Will racial tensions increase because of their presence? Will crime rates rise? What can be done about illegal immigrants? Because some people fear that the newest immigrants may not follow the pattern of upward mobility and Americanization established by the earlier immigrants, once again the cry is heard to close the open door.

Latino Immigrants Mr. Vasquez came to the United States in 1984. In 1986 he sent for his wife, Yolanda, and their two children. Back in Panama, the Vasquezes had been social workers and sought an even better education for their children. In the United States, Mr. Vasquez planned to obtain a high-paying job, save money, and send for his family. The Vasquezes now have a combined income of about $55,000 and live in their own $110,000 home, but success in America was by no means easy. Despite the fact that they had both been through college in Panama, Mrs. Vasquez had to work as a maid, and her husband as a parking lot attendant. For the Vasquez family life is still hard and the path to American citizenship is full of obstacles. Yet this Panamanian family feels that it will make it. They will become citizens and they will prosper.[4]

The United States has had a special relationship with Latin America since 1823, when the Monroe Doctrine declared that no foreign nation could establish any additional colonies in the region. This special relationship has not always been a friendly one, and many nations of Latin America have resisted what they view as unfair U.S. involvement in their governments and exploitation of their natural resources.

While European immigration was severely curtailed by restrictive legislation between the end of World War I and 1965, few restrictions applied to the people of Latin America. Nevertheless, relatively few Latin American immigrants came to the United States until after 1965, when immigration from all countries in the Western Hemisphere sharply increased. Immigration from South America and the Caribbean continues to grow.

Many immigrants from Mexico, Central America, South America, and the islands of the Caribbean are of Hispanic origin, Latinos, but they are a diverse group. (Puerto Ricans are not included in our discussion because as citizens of the United States they are not immigrants.) While Spanish is the dominant language of Latin Americans, those from Brazil speak Portuguese, those from Haiti speak French, those from Surinam speak Dutch, and those from Jamaica and other formerly British-ruled islands speak English. They come from over twenty different countries, each with a distinctive geography, history, and tradition.

The racial composition of those who come from Latin America is equally diverse. Immigrants from Mexico, for example, are mainly mestizos of Spanish and Indian ancestry; most of those from the Dominican Republic, Honduras, and Panama are racially mixed (black and white); nearly all immigrants from Haiti and Jamaica are black; from Cuba come some blacks but mainly whites; and most immigrants from Chile, Argentina, and Uruguay are white.

Immigrants from Cuba have come to the United States mainly as political refugees from Fidel Castro's authoritarian regime. The first group of Cubans sought refuge in 1959, after the Castro-led Communist revolution in Cuba. In 1965, Castro announced that all who wished to leave Cuba would be allowed to do so. President Lyndon Johnson reached an agreement with Cuba in which Castro agreed to a daily airlift of Cuban refugees.

In the spring of 1980, Castro announced that Cubans could again leave. From the Cuban port of Mariel, Cubans left for the United States in an assortment of vessels. However, those Marielitos, as they were called, were poor, uneducated, and unskilled, compared with the well-to-do anti-Communist group that fled Cuba when Castro rose to power. As a result, America gradually began to discourage further immigration from Cuba.

The poorest country in the Western Hemisphere is Haiti, a small nation that occupies one-third of the island of

These Haitian "boat people" were returned to Port Au Prince, Haiti, by the U.S. Coast Guard after their boat sank near the Bahamas.

Hispaniola in the Caribbean. Because it has long been politically unstable, with dictators replacing one another and persecuting their predecessors' supporters, many Haitians have fled to America.

While Haiti has sent many well-trained and well-educated immigrants to America, recent immigrants from Haiti have been among the poorest of the poor. While more than 200,000 Haitians reside in the United States, what to do about the recent Haitian exodus from their country has caused problems for the Reagan, Bush, and Clinton administrations. If Haitians are genuine political refugees, then America can become for them a land of asylum. But should America open its doors to Haitians who long to come to America to save themselves from abject poverty?

Asian Immigrants Nguyen Van Tran was, at age twenty-six, a skilled electronics technician and a lieutenant in the army of the Republic of South Vietnam. Nguyen was captured by soldiers from Communist North Vietnam and held for three years in a prisoner-of-war camp, all the while concealing his electronic skills. When the war ended, he managed to board a boat for Malaysia and, after spending two years as a refugee, finally arrived in Los Angeles in 1980.

Without family or friends, but with some government help, he started to improve his English and, before long, obtained a job in an electronics assembly plant. It was enough to support him and his new wife and child. After securing a community college degree in computer science, he and another Vietnamese technician and a Chinese engineer pooled their savings and opened a firm of their own. Within two years Integrated Circuits, Inc., employed three hundred workers, most of them illegal immigrant women from Mexico. In 1985 the company sold $20 million worth of semiconductors to IBM. Nguyen now calls himself George Best and drives a sleek Mercedes.[5]

The about-face that the United States government made in 1965 was more favorable to Asian immigrants than to any other group. Yet, just as it is somewhat misleading to refer to Latino immigrants without recognizing that these men and women represent a very diverse population, so must it be recognized that Asian immigrants also come from many nations. The Philippines, China, Hong Kong, Taiwan, India, Pakistan, and Korea contribute the largest number of Asian immigrants. Since the end of the Vietnam War, immigration from that country has increased substantially.

Among these immigrants are people who speak a variety of languages including Tagalog (Philippines); Indian dialects such as Hindi, Urdu, and Gujarati; and Farsi (spoken in Iran). Immigrants from the Philippines and and Vietnam are likely to be Catholic, whereas those from other countries of Asia might be Buddhist, Taoist, Confucian. Among Asian Indians there are Hindus, Muslims, Sikhs, Jains, and Zoroastrians.

Among the immigrants from Asia and the Pacific region are highly talented scientists and technicians who did not have to flee their countries. They could probably have done well enough if they had stayed where they were. Nevertheless, what they could have accomplished in their native lands was far less than what they hope to achieve in America.

But highly skilled workers were not the only Asians who sought safe harbor in America. The continuing displacement of men, women, and children as a result of the turmoil surrounding the end of the Vietnam War and the genocide (the killing of an entire racial or religious group) committed by the Pol Pot regime in Cambodia (1975) caused large numbers of the poor and oppressed to scramble for deck space on poorly equipped and unseaworthy vessels to escape from those lands. Under President Jimmy Carter these immigrants were admitted as political refugees, and their numbers grew rapidly. Most of these boat people lacked skills and education. They were fishermen, farmers, and laborers.

But for the highly trained as well as for the largely untrained, making a living in a new land proved to be a harsh experience. Even the well-prepared professionals had to start at a lower level in society than they had occupied at home, and they were often subjected to humiliation and discrimination. The ill-prepared had difficulty getting even the most menial jobs as dishwashers or floor sweepers. Nevertheless, life was better in America than it had been in the lands from which they came.

CONSEQUENCES OF IMMIGRATION REFORM

Along "Calle Ocho" (Eighth Street) in Miami's Little Havana, merchants post signs announcing that "English is spoken here." In Korea Town in Los Angeles, Korean merchants put up signs assuring shoppers that "Se habla español" (Spanish is spoken here). In Little Odessa, in the Brighton Beach section of Brooklyn, New York, there are many immigrants from the former Soviet Union, and signs in the Cyrillic alphabet outnumber those in English and Yiddish. Many schools in urban areas now offer classes in the students' native languages. While most bilingual education is Spanish-English, classes are also offered in French, Chinese, Tagalog (Flipino), and other languages.

It is said that these examples illustrate the changing face of America, but in fact, they replicate a model from the last century. Immigrant Jews on the Lower East Side in New York City developed a culture steeped in Yiddish. In heavily German areas it was sometimes hard to find anyone who could speak English or, for that matter, cared to do so. Although the pattern is familiar, many Americans who are themselves children of immigrants, remain uneasy about the diversity they see around them.

The immigration reforms of 1965 and subsequent adjustments had unintended consequences. The chief beneficiaries under the family reunification provisions were supposed to have been Europeans, especially those whose forebears had been shabbily treated during the World War II years when they sought refuge from Hitler's death camps. But in the 1960s Europe was prospering, and relatively few Europeans sought entry into the United States. Legislators were startled when, taking full advantage of the generous family reunification provisions of the law, overwhelming number of immigrants arrived from the poor countries of Asia and Latin America. Today about 90 percent of our immigrants come from Latin America, the Caribbean, and Asia.

In terms of numbers, today's immigration is about equal to that of 1900 to 1920, the peak immigration years. However, in those years immigrants made up about 1 percent of America's population. Today they constitute only about one-third of 1 percent. During those earlier years, most immigrants where white; today about 80 percent are people of color. Americans are being challenged to embrace a population more diverse than in the past.

Some Americans today are concerned that English as a national language may be lost, that there may be a greater loyalty to the land where one was born or to the ethnic group of which one is a part, than to the United States as a whole.

It would not be fair to attribute these changes to the immigration legislation alone. During the hundred years since the absorption of mass immigration from Europe, the world has become smaller. There are more contacts among the people of one nation with those of others. We are tightly bound together with economic, political, social, family, and cultural ties. Improvements in communication make it far easier to know what is going on in other parts of the world, and improvements in rapid transportation, make it easier to get where one wants to go. If automobiles, bananas, coffee, rice, sugar, clothing, even money and information, move across national boundaries, can people be far behind?

European immigrants, in generations past, were pushed into coming to America because of harsh political and economic conditions in their own countries or were pulled to America by real or perceived opportunities to improve their lives. The people of the so-called less developed countries today are, in many ways, where those of European countries were a hundred years ago and are both pushed and pulled to America. They are pushed from their native lands by harsh, authoritarian governments, dearth of economic opportunity, or political and religious persecution. They are pulled to America by the belief that economic improvement is surely awaiting them.

Moreover, no immigration legislation can anticipate events abroad. The distinguished scholar on ethnicity in America Nathan Glazer reminds us ". . . that we are more and more buffeted by the actions of others that we cannot control."[6] If Fidel Castro allows 100,000 Cubans to take to the seas, how shall the United States respond? If Vietnam expels hundreds of thousands of Chinese and other dissidents, does America have a responsibility to them? If Haitians seek to escape the squalid economic conditions and political violence in Haiti—the poorest country in the Western Hemisphere—if men, women, and children flee revolutions and civil war in countries such as Nicaragua or El Salvador, what should the United States do about it?

When Congressman Emanuel Celler introduced family preferences as an alternative to quotas based on national origins he confidently told Congress that "there will not be, comparatively, many Asians or Africans entering this country . . . since [they] have few relatives here."[6] Others echoed his views, but they were wrong. While it was expected that those from Europe who had the greater number of family members in the United States would benefit, the Europeans chose not to emigrate. Instead, extended families from non-European countries took advantage of the new immigration legislation, which appeared to welcome them.

An example of this is the case of a Filipino nurse who entered this country in 1972 with a temporary work permit and later obtained permanent resident status, enabling her to bring in her parents as immediate family members. A few years later, as a citizen, she sponsored her nine brothers and sisters. These brothers and sisters in turn secured entry for their spouses and children until a total of forty-five family members had reached the United States. Moreover, the children's spouses could in turn start new pyramids of immigration, beginning with their parents.[7]

Preference given to professionals opened the doors wider to Asian immigration than had been anticipated. While in 1973 fewer than 25 percent of all immigrants were in professional and technical fields, 54 percent of Asians and 67 percent of Filipinos were in this category. There were two unanticipated results of the immigration reform legislation: a great many skilled and professional people sought a better future for themselves in America; and their departure caused a "brain drain" in the very countries that most needed their skills. As the demand for medical care grew in the United States, so too grew the need for foreign doctors. As a result, by 1974 foreign-born physicians made up 20 percent of the American total: "There were more Iranian doctors, for example, practicing in New York City than in the whole of Iran."[8]

CITIZEN AND ALIEN

It took Armando Espinosa, an immigrant from Ecuador, nearly twelve years to decide to apply for American citizenship. "I am Ecuadorean in my blood and gut," he said.

Eventually, however, as his children became Americanized, and one was born in the United States and became a citizen at birth, Mr. Espinosa's attitude changed. It became obvious to him that "If people like me retain our allegiance to home and refuse to participate in electoral politics here, the lot of our race will never improve."[9]

In the 1990s only about 37 percent of eligible immigrants apply for U.S. citizenship; in 1946 about 67 percent did so. This decline in interest in becoming citizens has many causes. In the early days of this republic, crossing the Atlantic required a hazardous journey of many weeks, and immigrants were not likely to return to the land of their birth. The decision to uproot oneself was a permanent one. Today the jet plane makes any place on earth just a few hours away, and keeping in touch with family and friends requires pushing a few buttons on the telephone. Modern transportation and communication make emigrating from one's country of birth to America a more tentative decision than it once was.

Under the melting pot concept of immigration, immigrants were expected to assimilate and become citizens as soon as possible. The concept of multiculturalism encourages immigrants to retain and take pride in the language and culture of the land in which they were born. Some people maintain that this discourages immigrants from learning English immediately.

Because earlier immigrants thought of American citizenship as something worth striving for, they were willing to take the pledge required of naturalized Americans. However, becoming a citizen is no longer the badge of acceptance that it once was, and many immigrants are unwilling to prepare themselves for citizenship.

A legal immigrant requires both a visa and a green (now actually pink) card. The visa allows the immigrant to enter the United States legally. The pink card allows the immigrant to work in the United States. Resident aliens as well as citizens can enjoy the benefits of living in America. They can work, send their children to school, apply for welfare benefits, and avail themselves of the American legal system. Aliens as well as citizens must pay taxes and obey the law. Most aliens can be drafted into the armed services if military conscription is called. Because of these benefits and obligations, some immigrants put off becoming American citizens indefinitely, and some never do so.

But of course there are benefits to becoming an American citizen. American citizens can vote, whereas aliens cannot. Aliens are barred from holding most public offices, and some factories making weaponry for the American armed forces require their employees to be citizens. In some states, aliens cannot be certified as lawyers or doctors, and they are excluded from other professions as well. A few states limit an alien's right to own property and firearms. Other states deprive aliens of some welfare benefits, such as unemployment compensation.

American citizenship is available to legal immigrants. (Persons born in the United States, including children of aliens, are citizens at birth.) The process by which an alien becomes a citizen is called naturalization. It is not without its share of bureaucratic entanglements.

To become a citizen an immigrant must obtain the necessary application forms from the nearest INS office. The applications require the immigrant to answer a number of ambiguous questions such as: "Have you ever knowingly committed a crime for which you have not been arrested?" "Have you ever been an habitual drunkard?" "Have you ever practiced polygamy?" "Between March 23, 1933 to May 8, 1945, did you serve in or were you in any way affiliated with the Nazi Government of Germany?" "Have you ever been a member of the Communist Party?" When the application is completed, the applicant must mail the form to the INS and pay a fee of $90.

To be eligible for citizenship a person must be at least eighteen years of age and a legal resident of the United States for at least five continuous years.

Most applicants for citizenship must demonstrate that they have a reasonable command of everyday English. Exceptions include the infirm and the elderly. They must demonstrate that they are of good moral character and have some knowledge about American history and how the government of the United States works. For a $16 fee, applicants can take a test that may include questions such as: "During the Civil War, the President of the U.S. was_____." Or, "Where were the original 13 colonies?"

An interview follows the examination and applicants must bring with them the documents that support their application. The interview is often the most controversial part of the process of becoming a citizen. Some of the INS examiners are supportive, comforting and helpful. Others are arrogant, ask unfair personal questions, and otherwise rattle the applicant. If all goes well, over an eight-month process, the immigrant will be asked to report to a federal or state judge who makes the final decision. The immigrant then takes the following oath:

"I hereby declare, on oath, that I absolutely and entirely renounce and abjure all allegiance and fidelity to any foreign prince, potentate, state or sovereignty, to whom or which I have heretofore been subject or citizen; that I will support and defend the Constitution and laws of the United States of America against all enemies, foreign and domestic; that I will will bear true faith and allegiance to the same; that I will bear arms on behalf of the United States when required by the law; that I will perform noncombatant service in the armed forces of the United States when required by the law; that I will perform work of national importance under civilian direction when required by the law; and that I take this obligation freely without any mental reservation or purpose of evasion; so help me God."

Immigration is a federal responsibility which is shared by the President, the Congress, the departments of State, Justice, Labor, and Health and Human Services. Of these agencies it is the Immigration and Naturalization Service which bears major responsibility for carrying out federal immigration policy. It enforces the nation's immigration laws, processes applications for immigration and citizenship, inspects aliens for admission to the United States, deports those who are discovered to be here illegally. Aliens who commit a crime while in the United States, such as illegal gambling or selling narcotics, may be deported. However, according to FBI reports, while some aliens commit crimes, the crime rate for aliens is low.

This chapter has discussed mainly immigrants who legally enter the United States. But the number of illegal immigrants is growing, and the question of how best to deal with illegal, or undocumented, immigrants is becoming an important subject in the dialogue about developing a rational immigration policy.

ILLEGAL IMMIGRANTS AND POLITICAL REFUGEES

WE LIVE IN CAPTIVITY, WE MUST OBEY OUR masters. For us it is rough. We are all of us under a sufferation.

> An illegal West Indian
> Immigrant working in a
> Florida sugarcane field.[1]

Among the unanticipated consequences of the 1965 immigration reform legislation was a dramatic increase in the number of illegal immigrants who enter the United States in violation of its immigration laws. Before 1924, restrictions were few and, while there was some illegal immigration, it did not constitute a major problem. So widespread had illegal immigration become that President Ronald Reagan, in a fit of exasperation declared, "We have lost control of our borders."

WHO ARE OUR ILLEGAL IMMIGRANTS?

In Guadalajara, Mexico, Juan Manuel Fernandez worked as a mechanic in his uncle's repair shop, where he earned the equivalent of about $150 a month. At the age of thirty-two, after ten years as a mechanic, he decided to go into business on his own. In 1979, Juan crossed the border near El Paso, Texas, and settled in Gary, Indiana, where he established a successful automobile repair shop. He employs three other mechanics, two Mexicans and a Salvadoran. His wife, Luisa, no longer works. Their children speak English better than their parents, and they resist the idea of going back to Mexico.² The story of Juan and Luisa as illegals in America is obviously a story of success. But is this typical of the experiences of illegal aliens in America?

Illegal immigrants from the Western Hemisphere come from El Salvador, Guatemala, and Honduras, but most are from Mexico. Illegal immigrants from the Eastern Hemisphere come from Korea, the Philippines, Vietnam, and China. Today an estimated three million illegal immigrants, and perhaps more, are living in the United States. The exact number is unknown because they cannot be accurately counted. Americans often disagree about how to reduce illegal immigration.

The list of undesirable aliens takes up five pages in the United States Code. Some thirty-four categories of aliens are excluded from entering the United States as legal immigrants. They include the following:

- The mentally retarded and insane
- Sexual deviants
- Drug addicts, chronic alcoholics
- Those who have AIDS or are HIV positive, and those afflicted with other contagious diseases
- Paupers, beggars, vagrants, prostitutes, polygamists, and those who are likely to become public charges
- Stowaways and those who have invalid or forged visas, passports, or travel documents
- Those who are ineligible for citizenship
- Those over sixteen years of age who cannot read and understand some language or dialect
- Anarchists and Communists
- Those who have been convicted of a crime involving some moral offense, and those who have been imprisoned for five or more years

Most illegal aliens, however, are those who enter the United States before their turn is reached in their nation's quota. They may sneak across unguarded borders, carry forged visas and passports, or brazenly arrive with no documents at all. Some illegal immigrants arrive with legal documents for a temporary stay but remain long after their time limit has expired.

Illegal Immigrants from Mexico Fifteen-year-old Pedro, unwilling to serve in the Nicaraguan army, boarded a bus that would take him and thirty-two others to Matamoros, Mexico. The trip took about a month, but when Pedro arrived in Mexico, he was harassed by the Mexican police, who took his money and food and deported him to Guatemala. He began to think that he should have stayed in Nicaragua until he remembered his lifelong dream of living in America. Pedro reentered Mexico, where he was told that the best way to enter the United States was to swim across the Rio Grande and make his way to the church-run Casa Romero, a temporary refuge for young illegal aliens, where he would be safe. But Pedro faced a serious problem: if he reported to the United States Immigration and Naturalization Service, he would be put into a detention center; and he would soon be too old to stay at Casa Romero.[3]

The major source of illegal aliens, about 95 percent of unauthorized aliens or about 5,000 daily, are from Mexico, with which the United States shares a border. That border, some 2,000 miles in length, is unique in that it divides a rich, highly developed country, the United States, from a much poorer, developing country, Mexico. The minimum hourly wage in the United States is $4.25, about six times higher than the prevailing minimum wage in Mexico, so it is little wonder that working in the United States is attractive to Mexicans.

In 1849, following the war between the United States and Mexico, those Mexican citizens living in the territory acquired by the United States automatically became American citizens. Between 1876 and 1911, Porfirio Diaz (1830–1915) was the effective dictator of Mexico (except for the years between 1880 and 1884). Under Diaz, Mexico prospered. Railroads were built, foreign capital was attracted to the country, and the government was put on a sound financial basis.

Until the early twentieth century the flow of people across the border continued as Americans of the Southwest sought Mexican immigrants to labor on their farms and ranches and in their mines. The United States established the Border Patrol in 1924 in an attempt to regulate the flow of Mexican immigrants across the border.

Periodically American growers in Texas and California sought low-wage Mexican workers to help them harvest their grapes, lettuce, oranges, and other produce. Between 1942 and 1964 the bracero program encouraged Mexican laborers to work temporarily in the United States, where their labor was needed. During the twenty-two years of the program, about 4.8 million Mexican workers took part.

Braceros probably contributed to illegal immigration, because many of those who came on a temporary basis chose to stay. Also, since there were many more Mexicans who wanted to work as braceros than there were openings, many simply crossed the border illegally.

Allowing braceros to work in the United States was controversial from the beginning. The Mexican government was embarrassed by it because it implied Mexican inferiority. American ranchers and farmers of the Southwest wanted to continue employing the braceros because their labor was cheap, but labor unions in America were strenuously opposed to a program that encouraged employers to pay very low wages.

Employers who want to hire low-paid workers may violate the immigration laws and encourage undocumented workers to evade them. When economic conditions deteriorate, the illegal immigrants are no longer needed, but they may have lived in the United States for some time.

If high pay lures Mexican immigrants, both legal and illegal, rapid growth of the Mexican population at the rate of about 2.5 percent a year also propels them to the United States. About half the Mexican population is under the age of fifteen. With competition for jobs in Mexico becoming ever keener, America is the only alternative for the young with strong legs and stout hearts who risk their lives to cross the border into the United States.

Most of these illegal immigrants are young men who, odd as it may seem, have relatively more education than the average Mexican. Most of them are not so much unemployed as underemployed in Mexico—that is, they usually leave a job in Mexico in the hope of finding a better-paying one in the United States. Most of the illegal immigrants come from farms, but in the United States they seek employment in industry as often as in agriculture.

Illegal Immigrants from China In 1993, from Fuzhou in the Fujian province of China, a barely seaworthy freighter, the *Golden Venture*, carrying nearly three hundred desperate young people, ran aground about 200 yards from Rockaway Beach in Queens, New York, after a torturous journey that involved stops in Thailand, Kenya, and the Ivory Coast. In a panic, many of the Chinese passengers jumped from the ship into freezing waters while rescue workers from the New York Fire and Police Departments and from the Coast Guard sought to save them. All of the passengers were eventually taken to detention centers. Their future appeared grim, yet even as they were being hustled away, many of the passengers felt elated that they were in America.

A police helicopter searches the sea for survivors of the freighter Golden Venture. *The ship smuggling Chinese immigrants ran aground off a New York City beach on June 6, 1993.*

China, Vietnam, and the subcontinent of Asia and the Philippines, make up the second major and rapidly growing source of illegal immigration. Immigrants from Asia have become the new "jet set" as they arrive in 747s that land at various airports in the United States, where they thwart the immigration authorities by showing forged travel documents or by pretending that they are seeking asylum from political oppression. But as controls at the airports improve, many take to the seas, as did those in the *Golden Venture*. It is very difficult to intercept vessels carrying illegal immigrants over the vast oceans. Since 1991, more than 2,200 undocumented immigrants have come to America by sea.

In the People's Republic of China political as well as economic factors encourage emigration. As the Communist Party loosens its discipline, some want to escape the remaining constraints on their liberty by fleeing China. The upheaval that may follow the transfer of Hong Kong to the People's Republic of China in 1997 and of Macao shortly thereafter, will also increase pressures to emigrate. However, many Chinese seek to leave the land of their birth for economic reasons as well. In Fujian Province, on the China coast, from which many of the Chinese emigrants come, the average farmer earns $173 a year, and city dwellers earn about $367 a year. Even at the lower standard of living in China, supporting a family at these levels of income is nearly impossible.

Smuggling Chinese émigrés into the United States is a $3 billion a year industry. Crafty smugglers from the Chinese underworld—snakeheads, as they are called—promise that in return for a hefty fee of between $20,000 and $30,000 they will get their human cargo out of China and discharge them on American shores. On the *Golden Venture* there was one toilet, no running water, little food, little daylight, and the ever present discipline of agents of the snakehead, who sometimes beat the passengers.

Generally, snakeheads require a deposit of a portion of their fee. The rest they expect to collect from the labor of the illegal immigrant or from his or her family. The more relatives an immigrant has, the lower the deposit the snakehead is willing to take, since the chances of collection are so much greater. Threats, beatings, and even death await the illegal alien who fails to pay.

How to maintain America's traditional role as a haven for the oppressed, how to regulate a generous flow of legal immigrants, how to enforce the laws against illegal immigration, while safeguarding both the civil and human rights of immigrants is the current dilemma of America's immigration services. In an attempt to deal with these issues and to fine–tune the immigration reform legislation of 1965, Congress passed new legislation in 1980, 1986, and in 1990.

IMMIGRATION REFORM

A sixteen-member Select Committee on Immigration and Refugee Policy met in 1978 to study the precise impact of immigration on America and to recommend changes. Father Theodore Hesburgh, former president of Notre Dame University and the committee chairman, recommended that the basic legislation be kept intact but that a more generous policy toward legal immigrants be added as well as tighter controls over illegal immigration.

In commenting on the committee's report Father Hesburgh declared: "The essential recommendation was that America ought to open the front door to legal immigration a bit wider while shutting the back door to illegal immigration . . . we cannot accommodate everyone and must regain control of our borders."[4]

How to regain control of our borders was the subject of intense debate in Congress. In 1986, after several years of often emotional debate in Congress, the Immigration Reform and Control Act was passed and signed by President Reagan. This legislation sought to bring some order out of the chaos surrounding illegal immigration. The Immigration Reform and Control Act made it illegal for employers to hire illegal aliens under penalty of heavy fines and jail terms. In addition, the legislation offered amnesty (pardon) to those illegal immigrants who had entered the United States before January 1, 1982, and had lived in the United States continuously since then. However, for five years they would be ineligible for welfare, food stamps, and most other federal benefits. More funds were

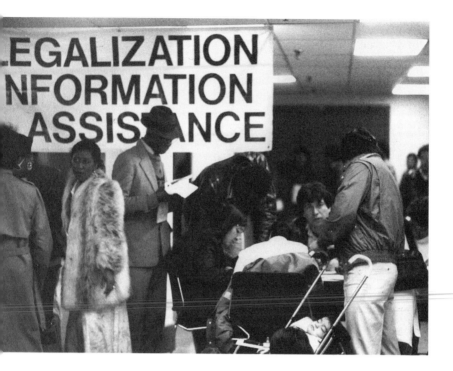

This is an INS office on May 4, 1988, the last day for undocumented aliens to apply for legal residency under the government's amnesty program.

appropriated for the Immigration and Naturalization Service, and the Border Patrol was significantly strengthened.

In 1990, President George Bush signed what he called "the most comprehensive reform of U.S. immigration laws in sixty-six years." The new legislation relaxed legal admissions requirements and offered admission to several new categories of immigrants. It increased the number of legal immigrants who could enter the United States between 1992 and 1994 to 714,000, excluding refugees.

The preference system in the new law admits the following people: (1) immigrants related to U.S. citizens and permanent resident aliens (71 percent); (2) immigrants with special skills (21 percent); and (3) immigrants from countries that were allotted few visas in the previous five years. The new legislation also set up a "temporary protected status" category for those fleeing disasters in their country of origin. They may stay until their countries are again considered safe.

The Immigration Act of 1990 establishes an annual visa lottery to create a greater diversity among immigrants. Illegal immigrants and those who wish to immigrate submit a plain sheet of paper with their name (the last name underlined) and date and place of birth. Lottery winners, if otherwise eligible, may receive a green card, which permits them to work legally in the United States. Ineligible to apply are immigrants and potential immigrants from Britain, Canada, China, the Dominican Republic, El Salvador, India, Jamaica, Mexico, the Philippines, South Korea, and Vietnam—countries from which many immigrants have already come to the United States.

Despite increased security along the border with Mexico, many illegal immigrants continued to enter the United States. Many still managed to find jobs, because the enforcement of penalties against employers remained lax.

The legislation of 1986, in the long run, failed to turn back the tide of illegal immigrants to the United States. However, after a slow start, about 3.7 million illegal aliens took advantage of the amnesty provision of the law, paid their application fees, and became legal permanent residents.

REFUGEES

In September 1991, soon after democratically elected President Jean Bertrand Aristide of Haiti was overthrown by the military, a sixteen-year-old girl in a tattered nightgown limped through the streets of Port-au-Prince. She had just been beaten and gang-raped by opponents of Aristide because her male cousin had supported the deposed Haitian president. Six weeks later she and her cousin fled by boat to the American naval base in Guantánamo, Cuba. After five months at the base, she was admitted into the United States, and is now a high school student in Boston. She is seeking political asylum but her case remains unresolved. She is one of a growing number of women seeking asylum on the grounds that they suffered persecution because they are women as well as politically oppressed.[5] The United Nations estimates that there are more than 23 million refugees from political oppression worldwide.[6]

By law, political asylum in the United States is granted to an individual with a genuine fear of persecution because of race, religion, nationality, or political opinion. Because of the politically motivated rapes of Muslim and Croat women in Bosnia, there is considerable debate over whether a category of asylum based on gender persecution should be created. Many Chinese ask for asylum in the United States to obtain relief from the oppressive regulations in China. Among these regulations is a very strict birth control policy that includes forced abortion and sterilization. This policy is meant to limit the number of children a Chinese couple can have. In 1989, President George Bush ordered that political asylum be given to all Chinese who seek refuge from "birth control persecution"—a claim that American authorities find it difficult to verify.

America's liberal asylum policies were established during the Cold War to admit refugees from the Soviet Union

Polish defector Leszek Kapsa, who jumped ship while it was docked in Cleveland, is granted political asylum, December 12, 1985.

and other Communist nations. These refugees were few in number in the past. Today, many more refugees claim asylum and disappear into the general population while the Immigration and Naturalization Service evaluates their claims—a process that can take years. The due process accorded U.S. citizens must be followed so that the rights of aliens are not violated. However, what about refugees whose ships are intercepted offshore? Do those refugees have such rights as well? In the case of *Sale v. Haitian Centers Council* (1993), the United States Supreme Court held that the policy of the Bush and Clinton administrations of intercepting fleeing Haitians at sea and returning them to Haiti without asylum hearings was not a violation of their rights. The only dissenter was Justice Harry A. Blackmun, who held that "a refugee may not be returned to his persecutors." The Supreme Court's decision is hailed by those who do not want very poor black refugees. It is condemned by those who feel that America is no longer being a haven for the politically oppressed and economically desperate. Critics note that white refugees from Castro's Cuba are always welcomed while black refugees from impoverished Haiti are refused entry.

During World War II, America made it very difficult for all but a few refugees from Hitler to enter the United States. Consequently, in 1980 Congress passed the Refugee Act, which attempted to establish a comprehensive national policy for refugees. According to this legislation the president sets an annual ceiling on the number of refugees who may enter the United States. Ceilings are set on the number of refugees from each part of the globe that are accepted. The Department of State's Bureau of Refugee Programs applies a priority system to decide which persons will be admitted. The highest priority is given to those in immediate danger of death.

In dealing with the world's millions of refugees, the United States tries to be generous. Yet, how to prevent the abuse of our liberal refugee provisions remains a problem. Not every person who claims refugee status deserves to be admitted. Among illegal immigrants who claim they are refugees are those who engage in terrorist activities in the United States. How does one assure that a refugee does not become threat to America? Moreover, affording all who claim refugee status with an appropriate and fair hearing often means that they will stay in America for years until their case is heard. In the meantime, many who claim refugee status disappear into ethnic enclaves in the larger cities of America where they cannot be found.

SHOULD THE OPEN DOOR BE CLOSED?

ON MAY 10, 1990, SHEIK OMAR ABDEL-Rahman, alleged leader of the terrorists whose explosives damaged a portion of the World Trade Center skyscrapers in lower Manhattan, was given a visa by the U.S. Embassy in Khartoum to travel to the United States. He settled in Brooklyn, New York.

The overwhelming majority of Muslims in the United States are law-abiding citizens who seek only to live in America in peace. Yet because a few are accused of terrorism, some Americans have begun to regard Muslim immigrants with hostility. Fear of terrorism, a limping national economy, the fact that most immigrants today are men and women of color are some of the factors that affect attitudes toward immigration. A New York Times/CBS poll taken in 1993 shows a continuing concern that there are too many immigrants in America.

Aggravating the anxiety about immigration are a number of misconceptions or myths about immigrants that many Americans harbor.

Myth: The number of foreign born as a percentage of the American population is greater now than ever before.
Fact: The percentage of foreign born in the United States population has fallen from 8.8 percent in 1940 to 6.8 percent today. The nation is not about to be overrun by immigrants.[1]

Myth: Most immigrants are illegal entrants into the United States.

Fact: While no one really knows how many illegals there are, it is estimated that no more than 300,000 people enter the country illegally each year. This number is large enough to constitute a problem; nevertheless, 76 percent of immigrants are legal. More than a million people are entering the United States legally every year. From 1983 to 1992, some 8.7 million legal newcomers arrived.[2]

Myth: Most legal immigrants who enter the United States have less education than native-born Americans.

Fact: Of African-born residents, 88 percent had a high school education or higher in 1990, as did 76 percent of Asian-born and 57 percent of Caribbean-born. These data compare with 77 percent of native-born who have a high school education or better.[3]

Myth: Most of the newest immigrants refuse or are at least reluctant to learn English.

Fact: Most of the newest immigrants are eager to learn English. The debate is largely how best to teach them. Some schools plunge the immigrant into an "English only" curriculum. Others take a bilingual approach in which they begin teaching children in their native languages while teaching English as well.

IMMIGRATION AS A GLOBAL PROBLEM

In the Brussels, Belgium, market square, Moroccans, Turks, Zaireans, Russians, Poles, Indochinese, Americans, and English mix with Belgians, who may be French-speaking Walloons or Dutch-speaking Flemish. Peruvian musicians entertain the crowds with their pipes and bearskin drums with music from the Andes mountains of South America.[4] This demonstrates that racial, ethnic, and cultural pluralism is no longer exclusively an American phenomenon. Many countries must wrestle with the problem of establishing a rational immigration policy.

- Sweden worries about the influx of refugees.
- France imposes random identity checks to detect illegal immigrants
- Under cover of darkness, North Africans take to fishing boats and desperately try to enter Spain.
- More political refugees seek asylum in Germany than in any other country in western Europe.
- Victims of "ethnic cleansing" in the former Yugoslavia clamor for admission to any country that will have them.

Immigration is a global problem that every major industrial nation has to deal with. *State of World Population*, an annual report issued by the United Nations, estimates that 2 percent of the world's population—at least 100 million people—are international migrants living outside the countries where they were born. On a global scale, immigration may be a problem not unlike that posed by the Goths, Vandals, and Franks, the migrant Germanic tribes who sought entry into the Roman Empire 1,500 years ago. Rome could not resist the flood of immigrants they called barbarians. Modern countries have tried to do so but have met with limited success.

Most countries of Europe have far stricter admissions policies than the United States. Most also give preference to applicants who have some previous ties with that country. Israel has the "law of return," according to which any Jew who wishes to immigrate to Israel is welcome. Germany gives preference to immigrants of German origin no matter how distant that relationship has become. Great Britain gives preference to those who were born of British stock. Some have suggested that the United States should take similar action and give preference to an immigrant stream closer in racial and ethnic character to the population of present-day America.[5]

IMMIGRATION IS A
NATIONAL PROBLEM

Setting immigration policy is the responsibility of the federal government. The president, in consultation with Congress, sets admission levels for refugees. The State Department issues immigrant and nonimmigrant visas, and its Bureau for Refugee Affairs helps eligible refugees come to America. The primary administrative focus of America's immigration administration rests with the Immigration and Naturalization Service of the Department of Justice. The Department of Labor's Employment and Training Administration coordinates immigration with the nation's labor needs. The Department of Health and Human Services reimburses states and localities for expenditures made on behalf of refugees and legal immigrants.

Congress and the House and Senate Judiciary Committees have jurisdiction over legislation having to do with immigration, citizenship, and refugees. The House and Senate Appropriations Committees are responsible for domestic and overseas funding of activities related to immigration. The Supreme Court has played an important role in interpreting immigration policy. In *Graham v. Richardson* (1971) the Court ruled that state welfare benefits may not be denied to aliens. In *Plyler v. Doe* (1982) the Court held that children of illegal aliens were entitled to equal protection of the law and must be allowed to enroll in public schools. In *Lewis v. Grinker* (1992) the U.S. District Court in New York held that pregnant women were entitled to prenatal care under Medicaid irrespective of their immigration status. It remains to be seen whether this ruling will be applied to other states as well.

IMMIGRATION IS A
STATE PROBLEM

The federal government of the United States sets immigration policies but the states in which the immigrants live carry out important aspects of those policies. Two-thirds of the immigrants who entered the United States between 1980 and 1990 went to just five states: California, New York, Texas, Florida, and Illinois. Thirty-four of the fifty states saw an increase in their foreign-born population. States like Vermont or Oklahoma, which in the past attracted few immigrants, now have to accommodate fairly large numbers of them.

Most states are hard-pressed to care for their immigrants. These newcomers, like other Americans, require police protection, for example. As the number of immigrants in any community grows, more police are needed. Immigrants, of course, are no more violent than other people, but they often live in crowded neighborhoods where additional police may be needed to curtail or prevent friction among individuals and groups. Moreover, the new arrivals may be ripped off by the unscrupulous who prey upon those who have little knowledge of American ways. Providing police protection is costly, and many state and local governments are having difficulty paying for it.

Although illegal immigrants are not entitled to most of the welfare benefits the state and federal governments provide, children of both illegal and legal aliens are expected to go to school. Indeed, it is in the schools where the local burden of helping immigrants often appears in dramatic forms. In some schools, classroom instruction and notices to parents must be available in many languages, from Spanish to Farsi. Providing school breakfasts and lunches, offering some medical oversight, purchasing appropriate instructional materials, hiring bilingual teachers—all compete for desperately needed funds. The federal government sets aside only $30 million a year for educating immigrant children. Since all schools whose recent immigrant populations amount to 3 percent of their total enrollment can apply for these limited funds, the amount that can be doled out to each school falls far short of its needs.

While Medicare and Medicaid are not available to illegal immigrants, some of them may require the services of the emergency room of the local hospital and usually will not be turned away. Illegal immigrants who are pregnant cannot be denied medical and prenatal care. These medical services can put considerable strain on a state's health care facilities.

The national government is also stingy with funds for states to help newcomers find jobs and housing, apply for a driver's or chauffeur's license, and provide interpreters. New immigrants often need such assistance to become self-sufficient.

Moreover, while illegal aliens are not eligible for most welfare benefits, their children born here are American citizens and, as such, are entitled to welfare, which is costly to provide. California, for example, spent $300 million dollars in 1993 for welfare payments to American-born children of illegal aliens. But when the governor of California, Pete Wilson, urged that American-born children of illegal aliens be denied citizenship, he raised a storm of protest. Nevertheless, because anti-immigration sentiment is growing in the nation, many Californians were sympathetic to Wilson's recommendation. Putting the governor's proposal into effect, however, would require an amendment to the Constitution—a lengthy and difficult procedure.

In 1994 Californians approved Proposition 187, which would deny education and nonemergency health benefits to illegal immigrants and their children. The courts may overturn Proposition 187, but its passage demonstrates Californians' frustration with their illegal immigrants. About 15 percent of all immigrants are refugees. Since they are in this country legally, they qualify for Medicare, Medicaid, and other welfare benefits. Since refugees often come to this country with few personal possessions and little money, they may impose a considerable drain on state funds.

Whether or not immigrants pay their fair share of taxes is a debatable point but most of the taxes they do pay goes to the federal government, and relatively little remains in the state to support their needs. Thus the federal government establishes immigration policy and gets most of the tax revenue immigrants pay, but the states and local communities must provide the funds to assist immigrants where they live. How to help the states and cities pay for these costs remains a pressing question.

IMMIGRATION IS A LOCAL PROBLEM

Some communities can feel threatened by what seems to be an uncontrollable problem. The following examples illustrate this problem.

- In the industrial New England city of Fall River, Massachusetts, many established residents are Portuguese-Americans. Today, however, Cambodians make up 4 percent of the city's population.
- About 6,000 Hmong refugees, descendants of a Laotian tribe who fought alongside American troops during the Vietnam War, live in Milwaukee, Wisconsin. The state is home to some 90,000 Hmong, or about 20 percent of the total Hmong in the United States.
- Mexicans, who constitute the largest immigrant group in America, live largely in California, Texas, New Mexico, Arizona, and Illinois.

- In Garden City, Kansas, residents share the local social facilities with immigrants, who make up 20 percent of the population.
- New York City receives the greatest number of Chinese immigrants.
- Francisco has a softball league made up entirely of Samoans.
- Most of Chicago's new immigrants come from Mexico.
- In Dearborn, Michigan, and in nearby Detroit, 200,000 Arabs hear the cry of the muezzin (Muslim crier) summoning the faithful to prayer. Other large centers of Muslim immigrants are New York, Chicago, Los Angeles, and San Francisco.

Because immigrants are concentrated in a few states and communities, the burden of helping the newcomers is unevenly distributed. Since immigration affects the nation as a whole, some means must be found to spread the burden more equitably. If that can be achieved, perhaps the xenophobia (fear of foreigners) that is so evident in some public opinion polls will diminish and immigrants' contributions to America will be appreciated.

Should U.S. immigration policy be changed? There are arguments for continuing an open policy of immigration and arguments for ending or severely limiting immigration.

THE DOOR SHOULD BE CLOSED

1. *Too many of the newest immigrants are unskilled.* George J. Borjas insists that the United States attracts relatively unskilled persons and concludes that it is time to close the door to immigration.[6] This viewpoint is heartily supported by Peter Brimelow, who maintains that the current group of immigrants has been "vastly larger, more unskilled . . . than was ever envisioned. There is no economic rationale for this influx . . . because labor is far less important" than it once was.[7]

2. *Immigrants take jobs away from Americans.* Donald Huddle, an economist for an anti-immigration lobby, maintains that newcomers make it more difficult for Americans to find jobs and that unemployment lasts longer because of legal and illegal immigrants. Even the jobs of skilled and educated Americans are threatened by immigrants. Immigrants with medical degrees or hospital experience, for example, make it harder for American doctors and nurses to get jobs in hospitals. Thus, American professionals as well as unskilled workers are forced to compete with recent arrivals who are generally willing to work for lower salaries.

3. *Immigrants keep wages down for all Americans.* The availability of immigrants who are willing to work for lower salaries encourages the growth of low-wage, low-tech industries, whereas it would be in the interests of the United States to develop high-wage, high-tech industry.

4. *America's newest immigrants receive more than their fair share of welfare benefits.* Recent newcomers are plagued by chronic poverty. Compared with immigrants of the 1950s and 1960s, many more of them depend on government aid and welfare. Governor Pete Wilson of California, in his reelection campaign, stressed the need to drastically curtail the flow of immigrants into the United States.

5. *Immigrants alter the ethnic character of the United States.* Those who favor stricter immigration limits believe that America as a racially white nation is threatened. Pat Buchanan, a former presidential candidate, believes that "High rates of non-European immigration . . . will swamp us all."[8] The Federation for Immigration Reform, an anti-immigration lobby, believes that without severe restrictions on immigration American customs and institutions will not be preserved. The historian, Arthur Schlesinger, Jr., writes:

"No one wants to be a Know-Nothing. Yet uncontrolled immigration is an impossibility; so the criteria of control are questions the American democracy must confront."[9]

6. *The newest immigrants adversely affect America's own minority groups.* According to the publication of the Federation for American Immigration Reform entitled *Immigration 2000, The Century of the New Sweatshop,* because immigrants are willing to work for substandard wages and under substandard conditions, often illegally and without benefit of unemployment or medical insurance, America's minorities find it especially difficult to compete for entry-level jobs.[10]

7. *The current rate of immigration aggravates America's environmental concerns.* Environmentalists, including members of the Sierra Club, are hostile to further immigration on the grounds that more immigrants use more natural resources and hasten the degradation of the environment. They point out that the U.S. population is growing faster than that of any other advanced nation and that this country no longer needs the population growth that immigrants provide. Former Colorado Governor Richard D. Lamm believes that the United States has set unsustainable models of population growth and resource consumption and that America must restrict immigration, "not totally, but dramatically."[11]

The evidence in favor of closing the door to immigration, which is only sampled here, is impressive. Yet those who want to keep the door open can offer equally impressive arguments. The latter essentially deny each and every assertion of those favoring a policy of closing the door on newcomers from abroad.

THE DOOR SHOULD BE OPEN

1. *Immigrants do not take jobs away from Americans.* Newcomers often take jobs that few Americans want.

Moreover, according to a study done by Richard Vedder, "Higher immigration is associated with lower unemployment. Vedder and his colleagues "found no statistically reliable correlation between the percentage of the population that was foreign-born and the national unemployment rate over the period 1900–1989, or for just the postwar era (1947–89)."[12]

2. *Immigrants create jobs.* One expert on immigration, Gregory De Freitas, insists that immigrants "increase the number of jobs."[13] Conservative presidential candidate and former Secretary of Housing and Urban Development Jack Kemp points out that "Immigrants are entrepreneurs; they are risk takers."[14] As entrepreneurs—that is, owners of their own businesses—they offer employment to recent immigrants, former immigrants, and native-born Americans as well. Some of their companies are large. Others are small businesses such as ethnic restaurants, grocery stores, and dry cleaning stores.

3. *Immigrants pay their fair share of taxes.* Julian Simon, an economist, calculates that during their first three decades in this country, immigrant families typically pay more taxes than their native counterparts do.[15] A report prepared by the Urban Institute estimates that the taxes paid by all immigrants, legal and illegal, exceed the costs of services they receive by $25 billion to $30 billion a year.[16]

4. *Immigrants do not rip off the welfare system.* According to Julian Simon, immigrants arrive young and healthy and use fewer services on the average than do native families. New waves of young immigrants do not receive expensive Social Security, Medicare, and other aid to the aged.[17]

5. *Immigrants contribute substantially to economic prosperity.* Immigrants need goods and services including housing, furnishings, food, and clothing. As an important group of consumers they contribute to the economy and in many communities they have been responsible for restoring economic well-being.

6. *The newest immigrants are becoming Americanized as rapidly as former immigrants.* Independence Day, Columbus Day, Thanksgiving, and other national holidays are still observed by native-born Americans and immigrants alike. The foods served at Thanksgiving dinner may be different, but the sentiments endure. Irrespective of the religious backgrounds of the newest immigrants, the spirit of the Christmas season still dominates the annual cycle. "Immigration does not substantially alter American institutions and culture. Rather, the immigrants absorb American ways and are absorbed into them."[18]

7. *Many immigrant children do well in school.* Ruben Rumbaut and Alejandro Portes studied the homework habits of the children of immigrants from seventy-seven countries. They found that immigrant children in the eighth and ninth grades devote between two and three hours a day to homework. American children in the same grades, on average, spend less than an hour a day on homework. As a result, the grades of immigrant children are often better than those of young native Americans.[19]

8. *Immigrants cannot be blamed for America's environmental problems.* If the people of the United States use up too much electrical energy, cut down too much timber, and deplete the soil, it is largely because of wasteful habits of resource consumption. America's affluence best explains environmental concerns. Moreover, population control does not stop at a nation's borders. It is a global problem that can be solved only through international cooperation. People are themselves an invaluable resource, and to deny admission to immigrants is to deprive the United States of an important resource.

"THERE SHALL BE OPEN BORDERS"

A five-word amendment to the Constitution, "There shall be open borders," has been proposed by the influential *Wall*

Street Journal. It stands in sharp contrast to the views of the Federation for American Immigration Reform (FAIR), which would impose a temporary moratorium (halt) on all immigration and severely curtail immigration after the moratorium is lifted. To FAIR the ideal appears to be the balance that existed in the 1920s, when the borders of the United States were essentially closed to immigrants. Between these two views stands a dizzying array of opinions that crisscross the political spectrum, making allies among those who otherwise have little else in common.

Moreover, economic arguments and statistical analysis seem to point in different directions. They can be made to serve those who wish to limit or close off immigration altogether, and they can serve equally well those who wish to allow the flow of immigrants to continue. "I have concluded," writes Nathan Glazer, an advocate of some modest restriction in the flow of immigrants, "that economics in general can give no large answer as to what the immigration policy of a nation should be."[20]

According to the press, most Americans favor some mild restrictions on immigration. Their opinion is based not on economics but on culture and ethnicity and a concern, despite evidence to the contrary, that the newest immigrants will not soon become a part of the American cultural scene. That most of the newest immigrants are people of color ignites a gut feeling that the newcomers will never be "like us." Yet Americans do not like to be accused of nativism. They prefer to retain their attachment to Emma Lazarus's "huddled masses yearning to breathe free."

America's immigration policy cannot be fixed once and for all. It must be fine-tuned frequently to respond to three essential questions.

How Many Immigrants Should This Nation Admit?

If, as the overwhelming body of evidence has it, immigrants do not take jobs away from Americans, then it would appear that the 900,000 legal immigrants currently admitted annually is not excessive. Since immigrants are overwhelmingly young people, they contribute to the costs of defense and the financing of our national debt. Their contributions to Social Security likewise mean that the current generations of Americans can rest assured that funds will be available for them through the contributions of immigrants.

A curtailment of the number of legal immigrants will cause many to attempt to enter the country illegally. If America is welcoming, pressures to flout the immigration laws may be diminished. It is not the overall number of immigrants that is of concern, but rather the concentration of immigrants in a relatively few of the nation's states and communities.

Who Should Be Admitted?

During the twentieth century there have been two major shifts in U.S. immigration policy. In 1924 the basis for admission was national origins. In 1965 the basis for admission shifted to family reunification and that remains, with some modification, the basis for most legal admission of immigrants to the United States.

Perhaps it's time to shift away from family entitlements to a priority for those who can bring needed skills to the American economy. Ben Wattenberg, a senior fellow at the American Enterprise Institute, urges the adoption of a "designer immigration" policy. He favors giving "liberty visas" to those men and women who lived in the former Communist countries and were not free to leave. He also favors preferential treatment for those who wish to leave the war-ravaged countries of the former Yugoslavia.[21] This would mean that the number of legal immigrants would be slightly increased, but America would be making a moral statement about the blessings of liberty. Wattenberg's policy would also add to the number of Europeans who are allowed to enter, and it would encourage immigrants more skilled than are those now coming from Latin America, the Caribbean, and Asia.

How Shall America's Immigration Laws be Enforced?

So long as there is a selection system there will be illegal immigrants. To the extent that legal immigration is increased, the number of those who either sneak into this country or extend their stay illegally might be reduced. But barring such an increase in legal immigration, what can be done about illegal immigration?

For years, many Mexicans illegally crossed the Rio Grande from Ciudad Juarez to the bustling city of El Paso, Texas. There, they took jobs that required them to care for children, do the laundry, mow the lawns, wash dishes, and mop the floors in restaurants and in the homes of affluent Texans. About 10,000 illegal Mexican aliens crossed the border daily and a sort of "fraternizing with the enemy" became common. But fear that jobs were being lost to Texans, many of whom were themselves of relatively recent Mexican origin, and a perceived increase in crime, led to a crackdown by the United States Border Patrol.

The deployment of hundreds of agents along the two-mile stretch has practically brought to a halt the human traffic in this area. But few are happy. The Mexicans are unhappy because they cannot take even the humble jobs that pay better than in their own country. There is no evidence that crime in El Paso has been reduced. And many Texans are upset because there is no one to perform the chores they need to have done. While some further policing of the border with Mexico may be necessary, do the American people really want to see a Berlin-like wall built between the two countries simply to keep hopeful immigrants out? Many Americans view the current wave of immigration with alarm, yet there are few who would suggest that a tactic fit only for a police-state be applied here. However, the problem of illegal aliens is a serious one for America.

To do nothing about illegal immigration reflects an unwholesome and intolerable disrespect for law. If a law cannot be enforced effectively perhaps there is something wrong with the law itself; if so it should be withdrawn or amended. Immigrant scofflaws cannot be permitted to live in the United States secure in the knowledge that American law is unable to reach them.

Among the steps to be taken are the more effective applications of fines, jail terms, and other sanctions against employers who flout the law by continuing to employ illegal aliens. Since the law was passed in 1986, the prescribed penalties have not been applied effectively. While larger employers should be forced to comply, those who employ illegal immigrants as household help should likewise be held accountable.

President Clinton's nomination of Zoe Baird as attorney general foundered because Ms. Baird had employed illegal aliens in her home and had not arranged for the appropriate taxes to be paid. While this is a widespread practice, it is unfair to the illegal alien worker, who does not build up Social Security and other benefits. But the task of filing the appropriate forms for part-time household help is so complex as to discourage those who are otherwise law-abiding citizens. The law making it illegal for employers to hire illegal aliens could be enforced more stringently, but the regulations could be simplified to make the tax forms less cumbersome.

The U.S. Commission on Immigration Reform, headed by Barbara Jordan, the former congresswoman from Texas, has suggested a computerized national employment registry of those aliens who are eligible to hold jobs. The registry would combine data from the Social Security Administration and the Immigration and Naturalization Service. If such a registry existed, employers would not have to ask aliens about their legal status, nor would they need to make a judgment based on race or nationality. Instead, by calling the registry and providing the Social

Security number of the prospective employee, employers could find out if the person they wish to hire is eligible for employment.

This proposal, however, has drawn much criticism from immigrant lobby groups and from the American Civil Liberties Union. They fear that the next step could be national identity cards or internal passports. Is such an invasion of privacy reasonable if it serves the interest of the nation by reducing illegal immigration? The Commission on Immigration Reform has proposed that the registry be tried at first in the states with the most illegal immigrants: California, Texas, Florida, New York, and Illinois. However, further tests in the courts are likely to follow before the procedure is put into use across the nation.

The U.S. Supreme Court has upheld as constitutional the dubious practice of intercepting shiploads of Chinese and Haitians and sending them away from U. S. shores without asylum hearings. The theory here is that they are not entitled to a hearing, since they have not actually landed. This practice will surely not help to solve the problem of how to determine which asylum–seekers merit compassion.

The Immigration and Naturalization Service is developing new and more efficient procedures for screening those who seek asylum. Among the proposals is a time limit on applying for asylum. There is no such time limit at present. There have also been proposals to withhold work

Zoe E. Baird testifies in 1993 at her Senate confirmation hearing for the post of U.S. attorney general. Baird was not appointed because of her failure to pay taxes on the wages of her employees, who were in the United States illegally.

permits for those who are in legal limbo until their cases are settled. A further restriction would be based on the concept of "country of first asylum"—that is, asylum–seekers who have passed through a country that has a procedure for providing asylum would be returned to that country, not to the country from which they are fleeing.

In Congress there is bipartisan support for new legislation that would increase the number of immigration officers who specialize in determining an asylum-seeker's status. If this is done, a system of "expedited exclusions" might be put into place in which a decision would be made on an asylum-seeker's status within a matter of days rather than years. However, the legality of this practice has yet to be determined. The asylum-seeker is entitled to be represented by an attorney, and a reasonable amount of time must be allowed for the lawyer to prepare a case. Moreover, these changes, if they are adopted, will affect only about 10 percent of asylum applicants—that is, those getting off the ship or plane, not those already arrived.

Unlike the illegal immigrants who come here in search of jobs, those who seek asylum are fleeing for their lives. About 78 percent of applicants for asylum come from Guatemala, El Salvador, the former Soviet Union, Haiti, the Philippines, mainland China, Pakistan, India, Cuba, and the Balkan nations. In 1993 about 250,000 applicants sought asylum in America.

• Wang Ke Jia from Fuzhou, China, arrives in Kennedy airport in New York City without documents. The immigration officer interviewing him has no idea on which flight he entered. Wang tells the officer that he paid $18,000 to a smuggler to help him escape. He is seeking refuge from China's harsh birth-control laws: Mr. Wang has four children; China punishes those who have more than two. This opening in American treatment of refugees was made possible during the administration of President Bush. If you were an immigration officer how would you decide?

- Yonis Elime Okiye, a handsome twenty-eight-year-old Somali dressed in a blue blazer and elegant Italian shoes, speaks English perfectly. He claims that his life is in peril from the warlords of Mogadishu. He fled to Yemen and from there to Milan, where he bought a fake Ethiopian passport and visa for $1,000. He destroyed these documents over the Atlantic. "It is my hope and I do expect that the American government will assist me out of a sense of humanity," he says. If you were an immigration official would you decide that Mr. Okiye is entitled to compassion?

Once in America, those seeking refuge cannot be arbitrarily put on the next ship or plane and sent home. Instead, in a matter of hours, after a cursory interview with an immigration officer, those who seek asylum may be on an American street. The unenviable task of determining which applicants are in peril and which are simply toying with America's laws, which tend to give refugees and asylum-seekers the benefit of the doubt, is in the hands of 150 immigration officers who specialize in these matters. To sort out the legitimate from the illegitimate asylum-seekers, the United States has a far smaller group of immigration officers than Australia, France, Germany, Holland, Norway, Sweden, Switzerland, or Britain. Because the officers are few in number and the circumstances of asylum-seekers are complex, many wait years before a legal determination is made of their status.

AFTERWORD

More important than tinkering with immigration laws are the choices immigrants themselves make once they get here. At one time when the "melting pot" concept was believed in, American institutions of business, labor unions, churches, synagogues, and especially schools communicated to immigrants the importance of choosing to become a citizen, learning English, understanding some of the unifying themes in America's history, taking pride in America's place in the world, studying the rudiments of how this democracy works, and participating in the democratic process.

One would not want to reinstate the "melting pot" concept of immigration with its often not-so-subtle racism and implied inferiority of immigrants' language and culture. In the fire of the "melting pot" the immigrants' pride in their native lands was shattered. However, if America may no longer be thought of as a "melting pot" perhaps it can be thought of as a garden in which immigrants establish roots that are then nurtured in the American soil. When thought of this way, the boat people of the *Golden Venture*, which brought Chinese illegals to America in 1993, may have more in common with the boat people of the *Mayflower*, which brought the Pilgrims of 1620, than we now think possible. The boat people who came on the *Mayflower* and those who came on the *Golden Venture* took the law into their own hands. The Pilgrims had no legal right to the land on which they put ashore and no specific authority to establish a government. The illegal Chinese flouted the law in a desperate attempt to improve their lives. Yet both put a painful past behind them, looked to a more hopeful future and came to America in search of greater opportunities for themselves and those who followed them.

The message that needs to be made loud and clear is that the immigrant is welcome here, that the native language need not be a source of shame, that the children of newcomers may retain their native tongue, but that Americans at their best look for what keeps them together, not what pulls them apart. Learning English, becoming citizens, respecting the law, participating in the political dynamics of the nation are worthy goals if the immigrant is to leave to future generations an American heritage upon which to build.

GLOSSARY

alien a person who lives in a country other than the one in which he or she was born but who is not a citizen of the new country.

anti-Semitism hostility to Jews.

asylum temporary refuge offered those who are politically threatened.

bilingualism the encouragement offered immigrants to retain their native languages while learning English. In schools, children are taught in their native languages until they can make a transition to English instruction. Notes to parents are sent in native languages.

bracero program a program launched during World War II designed to provide American farmers in the Southwest with immigrant Mexican labor.

citizen a person who swears allegiance to a country. In the United States, a person may become a citizen through birth in this country or by naturalization (see below).

conquistadores Spanish conquerors of Peru, Mexico, and the southwestern United States. They laid the basis for early Hispanic immigration.

coyote a person who, for a payment, smuggles illegal Mexican immigrants across the U.S. border.

cultural pluralism racial and national diversity.

Ellis Island the main point of entry for immigrants, mainly from southern and eastern Europe, between 1880 and 1924. Now a museum.

emigrant a person who leaves his or her country to live in another.

green card   a document authorizing an alien to work in the United States.

illegal alien   a person who has entered the country in violation of immigration laws.

immigrant   a person who comes to another country in order to live there.

Immigration and Naturalization Service (INS)   the government bureau that administers U.S. immigration policy.

kaleidoscope   a concept similar to "mosaic" except that it suggests that the mix of immigrant nationalities is ever changing.

melting pot   a vision of immigration which suggests that immigrants give up the culture of their homeland and become Americanized.

migrant   a person who moves from one place to another, usually on a temporary or seasonal basis.

mosaic   a concept that suggests that America is a land in which immigrants can become Americanized while retaining the language, religion, and culture of their homeland.

multiculturalism   the idea that America is a country in which immigrant groups are encouraged to retain their native culture and language.

national origins quota   policy according to which America's ethnic mix should be what it was in 1890 or 1920, when countries of northern and western Europe were allowed to send more immigrants to America than were the nations of eastern and southern Europe.

nativism   the policy of giving preference to native inhabitants rather than to immigrants.

naturalization   the process by which an alien becomes a citizen.

padrone   a person who, for a fixed fee, supplies contract laborers, usually Italian, for American industry.

pale of settlement   areas of czarist Russia (Poland, Lithuania, White Russia, Ukraine, Bessarabia, Crimea) where Jews were permitted to establish permanent residence. Certain

Jews were given special permission to live elsewhere. Those who lived outside the pale of settlement did so at their own risk.

passport   an official document authorizing a person to travel abroad.

pogrom   the organized terrorization and murder of Russian Jews.

promised land   America, which was viewed by some immigrants as the land in which they were destined to live. The metaphor comes from the biblical reference to ancient Palestine as the promised land.

refugee   a person who flees to another country for safety.

safety valve   a term used to describe the role of emigration in relieving the pressure on a country to provide for the economically distressed.

snakehead   a person who, for payment, smuggles illegal Chinese immigrants into the United States.

visa   an official document, usually attached to a passport, indicating that a person may enter the granting country. A passport is official permission to leave; a visa is official permission to enter.

Source Notes

PREFACE

1. Quoted in David M. Brownstone, Irene M. Franck, and Douglas L. Brownstone, *Island of Hope, Island of Tears* (New York: Rawson, Wade, 1979), p. 199.
2. Quoted in Pamela Reeves, *Gateway to the American Dream* (New York: Crescent Books, 1991), p. 68.
2. Alan Wolfe, "The Return of the Melting Pot," *New Republic*, December 31, 1990, p. 27.
3. Ruben G. Rumbaut, "Passages to America: Perspectives on the New Immigration." In Alan Wolfe, ed., *America at Century's End* (Berkeley: University of California Press, 1991), p. 210.
4. "Immigrants Less Welcome in 1990s America," *Gallup Poll Monthly*, March 1992, p. 6.
5. Seth Mydans, "Poll Finds Tide of Immigration Brings Hostility," *New York Times*, June 26, 1993.
6. Robert D. McFadden, "Immigration Hurts City, New Yorkers Say in Poll," *New York Times*, October 18, 1993.

CHAPTER ONE

1. "What Is It Like to Be an Immigrant in America?" *Wall Street Journal*, July 3, 1990.
2. John Hope Franklin, *From Slavery to Freedom* (New York: Knopf, 1966), p. 73.
3. Clinton Rossiter, ed., *The Federalist Papers* #42 (New York: New American Library, 1961), p. 269.

4. Bernard Bailyn, *The Peopling of British North America* (Madison: University of Wisconsin Press, 1986), p. 5.

CHAPTER TWO

1. David Gonzales, "New Country Is Like Prison to Asenhat," *New York Times*, April 30, 1993.
2. Wayne Andrews, ed., *Concise Dictionary of American History* (New York: Scribner's, 1962), p. 442.
3. Hasia R. Dinar, *Erin's Daughters in America: Irish Immigrant Women in the Nineteenth Century* (Baltimore: John Hopkins University Press, 1983), p. 73.
4. Martha Kaarsberg Wallach, "German Immigrant Women," *Journal of German-American Studies* 13, no. 4 (Winter 1978), No. 4, pp. 104–5.
5. Maldwyn Allen Jones, *American Immigration* (Chicago: University of Chicago Press, 1967), p. 135.
6. Salvatore J. Lagumina, *The Immigrants Speak: Italian-Americans Tell Their Story* (New York: Center for Migration Studies, 1979), pp. 190–91.
7. Quoted in Leonard Dinnerstein and David M. Reimers, *Ethnic Americans: A History of Immigration* (New York: Harper and Row, 1988), p. 44.
8. Uri D. Herscher, *The East European Jewish Experience in America* (Cincinnati: American Jewish Archives, 1983), pp. 140–41.
9. Quoted in Richard A. Easterlin et al., *Immigration* (London: Belknap Press, 1982), p. 85.
10. Quoted in Henry Steele Commager, ed., *Immigration and American History: Essays in Honor of Theodore C. Blegen* (Minneapolis: University of Minnesota Press, 1961), p. 28.
11. *Ibid.*, p. 35.
12. Israel Zangwill, *The Melting Pot* (New York: Arno Press, 1975), pp. 184–85.
13. Lawrence H. Fuchs, The American Kaleidoscope: Race,

Ethnicity, and the Civic Culture (Hanover, N.H.: University Press of New England, 1990), pp. 275–76.

CHAPTER THREE

1. Gordon Thomas and Max Morgan Witts, *Voyage of the Damned* (New York: Stein and Day, 1974), p. 281.
2. Michael N. Dobkowski, ed., *The Politics of Indifference: A Documentary History of Holocaust Victims in America* (Washington, D.C.: University Press of America, 1982), p. 280.
3. Quoted in Leonard Dinnerstein and David M. Reimers. *Ethnic Americans: A History of Immigration*. 3rd Edition (New York: Harper and Row, 1988), p. 35.
4. Quoted in Maldwin Allen Jones, *American Immigration* (Chicago: University of Chicago Press, 1960), pp. 152–53.
5. Quoted in Richard A. Easterlin, *Immigration* London: The Belknap Press of Harvard University, 1982), p. 97.
6. David S. Wyman, *The Abandonment of the Jews: America and the Holocaust* (New York: Pantheon Books, 1984), p. x.
7. Quoted in Francesco Cordasco, *The New American Immigration* (New York: Garland Publishing, 1987), p. xiv.

CHAPTER FOUR

1. Stanley Karnow, "In Orange County's Little Saigon Vietnamese Try to Bridge Two Worlds," *Smithsonian*, August 1992, pp. 34–35.
2. Lawrence H. Fuchs, *The American Kaleidoscope: Race, Ethnicity, and the Civic Culture* (Hanover, N.H.: University Press of New England, 1990), pp. 275–76.
3. Quoted in Richard Easterlin, *Immigration* (London: The Belknap Press of Harvard University, 1982), p. 103.
4. Evelyn Nieves, "Newcomers Find success Despite Barriers," *New York Times*, June 8, 1993, p. A1.

5. Alejandro Portes and Ruben G. Rumbaut, *Immigrant America: A Portrait*, (Berkeley: University of California Press, 1990), pp. 3 -4.

6. Nathan Glazer, ed. *The New American Immigration: A Challenge to American Society*. San Diego: San Diego State University Press, 1988, p. 7.

7. Quoted in Ruben Rumbaut, "Passages to America: Perspectives on the New Immigration." In Alan C. Wolfe, ed., *America at Century's End* (Berkeley: University of California Press, 1991), p. 214.

8. Maldwyn Allen Jones, *American Immigration*. 2nd Edition. (Chicago: University of Chicago Press, 1991), pp. 270–71.

9. *Ibid.*

10. Deborah Sontag, "Immigrants Forgoing Citizenship While Pursuing American Dream," *New York Times*, July 25, 1993, p. 1.

CHAPTER FIVE

1. Quoted in Paul Glastris, "Coming to America," *U.S. News and World Report*, Vol. 114, No. 24, p. 26.

2. Alejandro Portes and Ruben G. Rumbaut, *Immigrant America: A Portrait*. (Berkeley: University of California Press, 1990), pp. 1–2.

3. Phillip Anastos, *Illegal: Seeking the American Dream* (New York, Rizzoli, 1991), p. 60.

4. Quoted in Francesco Cordasco, *The New American Immigration* (New York: Garland Press, 1987), p. xix.

5. Deborah Sontag, "Asking for Asylum in U.S.: Women Tread New Territory," *New York Times*, September 27, 1993.

6. John Darton, "U.N. Faces Refugee Crisis That Never Ends," *New York Times*, August 8, 1994.

7. Tim Weiner, "Pleas for Asylum Inundate System for Immigration," *New York Times*, April 25, 1993.

8. *Ibid.*

CHAPTER SIX

1. Peter D. Salins, "Take a Ticket," *New Republic*, December 27, 1993, p. 13.
2. David Alkman and David S. Jackson, "Not Quite So Welcome Anymore," *Time*, Vol. 142, No. 21, 1993, p. 10.
3. "The Numbers Game," *Time*, p. 14.
4. George Melloan, "Closing Europe's Doors Will Have a Cost," *Wall Street Journal*, June 7, 1993, p. A15.
5. See Nathan Glazer, "The Closing Door," *New Republic*, p. 18.
6. George J. Borjas, *Friends or Strangers: The Impact of Immigration on the U.S. Economy* (New York: Basic Books, 1990), p. 18.
7. Julian Simon, "Why Control the Borders?" *National Review*, February 1, 1993, p. 33.
8. Quoted in Julian Simon, "Why Control the Borders?" p. 27.
9. Arthur Schlesinger, Jr., *The Disuniting of America: Reflections on a Multicultural Society* (New York: Norton, 1992), p. 121.
10. See Federation for Immigration Reform, *Immigration 2000: The Century of the New American Sweatshop*, Washington, D.C.: 1992.
11. Richard D. Lamm, "The Ethics of U.S. Immigration Policy in an Overpopulated World," in Robert W. Fox and Ira H. Mehlman, eds., *Crowding Out the Future: World Population Growth, U.S. Immigration, and Pressures on Natural Resources* (Washington, D.C.: Federation for American Immigration Reform, 1992), p. 25.
12. Richard Vedder, "Immigration Doesn't Displace Natives," *Wall Street Journal*, March 28, 1994.
13. Quoted in Larry Rohter, "Revisiting Immigration and the Open Door Policy," *New York Times*, September 19, 1993.

14. Quoted in Albert R. Hunt, "Demagoging the Immigration Issue" *Wall Street Journal*, July 7, 1994, p. A13.
15. Quoted in Rohter. "Revisiting Immigration."
16. Quoted in Hunt, "Demagoging." Julian L. Simon, "The Nativists are Wrong," *Wall Street Journal*, August 4, 1993.
18. See Simon, "Why Control the Borders?" p. 28.
19. See Editorial, *Wall Street Journal*, March 18, 1994.
20. Glazer, "Closing Door," p. 17.
21. Ben J. Wattenberg quoted in Julian Simon, "Why Control the Borders?" pp. 30–32.

SUGGESTED READING

Anastos, Phillip, and Chris French. *Illegal: Seeking the American Dream*. New York: Rizzoli, 1991.

Conover, Ted. *Coyotes: A Journey through the Secret World of America's Illegal Aliens*. New York: Vintage, 1987.

Fuchs, Lawrence H. *The American Kaleidoscope: Race, Ethnicity, and the Civic Culture*. Hanover, N.H.: University Press of New England, 1990.

Glazer, Nathan, ed. *The New American Immigration: A Challenge to American Society*. San Diego: San Diego State University Press, 1988.

Glazer, Nathan, and Daniel Patrick Moynihan. *Beyond the Melting Pot*. Cambridge, Mass.: M.I.T Press, 1963.

Handlin, Oscar. *A Pictorial History of Immigration*. New York: Crown, Inc. 1972.

Handlin, Oscar. *The Uprooted*. Boston: Little, Brown, 1973.

Jones, Maldwyn. *American Immigration*. 2d ed. Chicago: University of Chicago Press, 1992.

Lamm, Richard, and Gary Imhoff. *The Immigration Time Bomb*. New York: Dutton, 1985.

Portes, Alejandro, and Ruben G. Rumbaut. Immigrant America: *A Portrait*. Berkeley: University of California Press, 1990.

Reeves, Pamela. *Gateway to the American Dream*. New York: Crescent Books, 1991.

Reimers, David M. *Still the Golden Door: The Third World Comes to America*. New York: Columbia University Press, 1985.

Schlesinger, Arthur M., Jr. *The Disuniting of America: Reflections on a Multicultural Society.* New York: Norton, 1992.

Sowell, Thomas. *Ethnic America.* New York: Basic Books, 1991.

INDEX

Page numbers in *italics* indicate illustrations.